Grappling – Effective Groundwork Techniques

Warning

This book contains some techniques that can be dangerous and must only be practiced under the supervision of a qualified trainer or instructor. The author and the Publishers cannot be held responsible for any injuries that might ensue.

This book has been written using exclusively the male form of the personal pronoun. Of course, for reasons of simplicity this should be understood to include the female form as well.

Christian Braun

Grappling
Effective Groundwork Techniques

Meyer & Meyer Sport

Original title: Grappling - Effektive Bodentechniken
© Meyer & Meyer Verlag, Germany 2005

British Library Cataloguing in Publication Data
A catalogue record for this book is available from the British Library

Christian Braun
Grappling - Effective Groundwork Techniques
Oxford: Meyer & Meyer Sport (UK) Ltd., 2007
ISBN 13: 978-1-84126-212-3

© 2007 by Meyer & Meyer Sport (UK) Ltd.
Aachen, Adelaide, Auckland, Budapest, Graz, Johannesburg,
New York, Olten (CH), Oxford, Singapore, Toronto
Member of the World
Sports Publishers' Association (WSPA)
www.w-s-p-a.org
Printed and bound by: B.O.S.S Druck und Medien GmbH, Germany
ISBN 13: 978-1-84126-212-3
E-Mail: verlag@m-m-sports.com
www.m-m-sports.com

CONTENTS

Foreword

"Christian is generally a good boy, but he likes to brawl and tussle often, which puts his classmates in danger." This is how my teacher described me in my very first school report.

Right from a young age, brawling and tussling (not fighting) with others fascinated me. But it wasn't until I was 18 years old that various circumstances allowed me to come into contact and to begin practicing the Martial Arts (then Jiu-Jitsu). The old Jiu-Jitsu program (prior to 2000) practiced then by the Deutscher Ju-Jutsu Verband e.V., (German Jiu-Jitsu Union) (called DJJV throughout this book) did not include very many groundwork techniques, so therefore I was on the lookout, being already a Black Belt in Jiu-Jitsu, for a more comprehensive training method.

In the 90s, and even today, it could be said that in order to be successful in the competitive Martial Arts that are carried out almost without rules (e.g., "Vale Tudo" and "Pride"), one had to have had specialist training in groundwork. Fighters from the Family Gracie camp (Gracie Jiu-Jitsu) dominated the competition arena for many years. Above all they were dominant in those fights where there was no time limit on the length of the competition. Because these fights went on sometimes for hours, and were considered boring for the spectators, a time limit was introduced. Some of them were so good that even a considerably heavier opponent did not have a chance against them.

As a result of the knowledge gained particularly from these championships, the training and grading program of some of the systems and styles of Martial Arts were changed, as happened in the DJJV. In the Jiu-Jitsu grading program, there is an element of groundwork contained in each phase. This is where experienced trainers such as Joachim (Joe) Thumfart and Achim Hanke have employed their expertise. Even styles such as Wing Tsun (sometimes spelled differently) developed an 'anti-groundwork' program. This program contains more striking and kicking in groundwork than techniques for escape and completing actions, as taught in for example Luta-Livre or Brazilian Jiu-Jitsu (BJJ).

An experienced groundwork fighter will always try to keep in mind to be as close as possible to his opponent and to control the extremities, so that it is difficult to effectively injure him by striking or kicking. In the meanwhile I have met more and more WT (spelled also in other ways) trainers and students, who wish to improve their abilities in this.

Many of the Thai kick-boxers, who take part in these tournaments (for example "Vale Tudo" or "Pride"), have extended their program of techniques by employing groundwork techniques. Groundwork specialists have also learned Thai or kickboxing so that fights are now more evenly balanced. In my opinion, the types of sport that come into question as being particularly good for ground fighting are Brazilian Jiu-Jitsu (Gracie Family and Machado), the Sambo style (Russian self-defense) and Luta-Livre (Brazilian wrestling).

In the first place, the difference between BJJ and Luta-Livre is that in BJJ you wear a Gi (exercise outfit (suit) like in Judo) and in Luta-Livre only a T-shirt and short pants. This means that many of the techniques (grips, strangleholds) that can only be carried out when wearing a suit, cannot be used on an opponent who is wearing a T-shirt and short pants. As long as the opponent is wearing a Gi it is easier to grab hold of him and pin him down. Without a Gi and with sweaty hands and arms, there are only a few feasible grips that can be used. The fight without the Gi is more dynamic and the fighter has to think one or two steps in advance of the opponent to be able to plan a counter movement.

It is therefore important that when exercising, the techniques should be practiced in a manner so that they can be automatically used (i.e., as a reflex). Whenever thought has to be made before employing one or the other counter movement, it will always be more difficult to be successful.

Other than this, I see a lot of similarity in many of the concepts and techniques. Myself, I prefer to train without a Gi (because for me, also being a Jiu-Jitsuka, it is more realistic this way when thinking about self-defense). This is why I prefer Luta-Livre. Training, wearing a Gi has also lots of advantages, because one learns how to use clothing for actions (e.g., the jacket). A fighter, who starts off learning without putting on the Gi, will probably never learn these techniques. These techniques with the Gi are in any case mandatory in the contemporary Jiu-Jitsu grading program.

I first came into contact with the extensive concept of ground fighting in 1996 through Thomas Cruse (then the Vice-President of Progressive Fighting Systems). Tom is the holder of a Black Belt in Brazilian Jiu-Jitsu and played a big role in impressing me in those days. Together, with others mentioned in the next paragraph, he has demonstrated exercise fights for participants on courses.

After this meeting, I looked around for specialist courses and up to now I have been able to train together with some top trainers. Amongst others, I mention Roy Harris (holder of the Dan in BJJ), August Wallén (Head Coach of Shootfighting) and nowadays I am with Andreas Schmidt, the Head Coach of the European Luta-Livre Organization (www.luta-livre.de). I have also attended several courses run by his instructor – Daniel Dane as well as many courses run by Achim Hanke (7th Dan Jiu-Jitsu, 5th Dan Judo). I have also been able to learn a lot in this area from Joachim (Joe) Thumfart – the current Technical Director of the German Ju-Jutsu Union (www.ju-jutsu.de). All those, who I have mentioned are excellent instructors who I can wholeheartedly recommend.

This book is aimed at students of the arts and instructors, who wish to improve their ability in groundwork or practice the techniques.

Any suggestions or ideas for improvements can be sent to me via e-mail at christian.braun@fight-academy.eu

May I wish the reader lots of fun working through this book and offer the following maxim "Absorb what is useful". These words stem from the legendary Bruce Lee, the founder of Jun Fan Gung Fu and Jeet Kune Do and in the meanwhile it has also become my maxim.

Frankenthal, Spring 2006

Christian Braun

christian.braun@fight-academy.eu

A Word of Thanks

I would like to give a special thanks to my students Gunther Hatzenbühler, Tobias Hörr, Gabriele Rogall-Zelt and my student and training partner as well as friend - Waldemar Wodarz, for their support in producing this book.

Gunther Hatzenbühler

Tobias Hörr

Gabriele Rogall-Zelt

Waldemar Wodarz

1   Breakfalls

The breakfalls are presented each time in two steps. The first step is for the beginner and shows getting ready to practice carrying out the fall. The second step shows the fall being executed from a standing position.

Forward Roll

- Getting ready

- From a standing position

Backward Roll

- Getting ready

- From a standing position

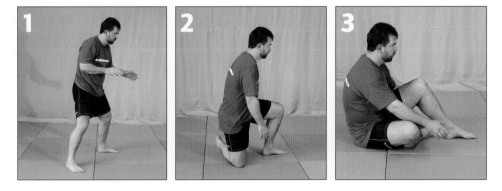

Falling sideways

- Getting ready

- From a standing position

Falling forwards

- Getting ready

- From a standing position

Falling backwards

- Getting ready

- From a standing position

2   Specific Gymnastics

2.1   Spider

1. D is crouched down on all fours so that his knees are very close to the ground. Using this position, D moves along over the floor like a spider.
2. With a turn (face looking at the floor or the ceiling) D brings his right leg under the other one...
3. ...and turns over.

4. In order to turn back over again, D pulls his left leg...

5. ...through under the other...

6. ...and is back in the posture on all fours.

2.2 Crab/Caterpillar

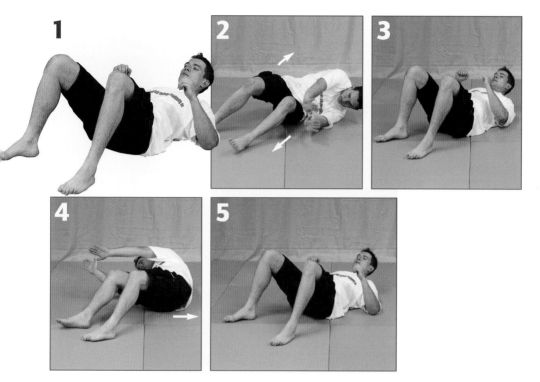

1. D is lying on his back with both legs propped forwards...
2. ...and pushes his bottom to the right (45° to the rear). At the same time D makes movements with his arms as if he wanted to (for example) push A's knee away with his hands.
3. He then resumes the starting position.
4. D pushes his bottom to the left (45° to the rear). At the same time D makes movements with his arms as if he wanted to (for example) push A's knee away with his hands...
5. ...and then resumes his starting position again.

2.3   Lifting up Using the Bridge

D is lying on his back with both of his legs pulled up against his bottom and pushes his hips upwards, turns onto one shoulder and touches the ground with the arm of the other shoulder.

2.4 Changeover from the Bridge to the Spider

D is lying on his back with both of his legs pulled up against his bottom and pushes his hips upwards, turns onto one shoulder and touches the ground with the arm of the other shoulder. D turns over further and is now in the Spider position.

2.5 Preliminary Exercise for the Guard Position

D is lying on his back with his legs lifted and bent up at right angles to the floor. From this position D rotates his lower legs inwards and outwards.

2.6   Candle

1

3

D is lying on his back with his legs lifted and bent up at right angles to the floor. From this position he lifts his legs upwards further to the rear and forms a candle. As he lifts his legs up in the air, D can turn his hips to increase the effect.

3   Training Tips

- First, only the technical sequence should be practiced. Here, the partner offers no resistance. Only when everything begins to become natural should the partner offer resistance (70%) in order to see whether the technique works.

- The techniques should be "tried out" on somebody, who is technically not as good (a beginner with some experience) and lighter. Here, one can use what has been learned without being confronted with effective counter-techniques. If the partner is more experienced, and maybe also stronger, the danger exists that one will consider the new techniques as ineffective, because they cannot be applied, and no longer practices them.

- When a technique doesn't succeed in training, because one doesn't understand the movements, it can be advisable to make a short pause, for example get something to drink or go to the toilet. In this case, a block between the two halves of the brain may be the cause of confusion. Both halves of the brain have their own function. With many people, the left half of the brain controls the functions of: logic, analysis, speech, numbers, linearity and others. The right half of the brain is responsible for rhythm, area-perception, fantasy, etc. In order to complete an exercise sequence, both halves of the brain must work together. In stressful situations or with overload (which can also be stressful), it is possible that this is not the case. The legs and arms are crossed during the movements in the exercise sequences, and this action can free up the blockage. This " technique" can also be applied to everyday problems. In the area of kinesiology, there are many exercises that are conducive to both halves of the brain working together better.

- Also the double-stick training in Kali (Arnis and Eskrima) contributes to the improvement of these abilities. When the complex exercises, that require use of both halves of the brain, are often repeated, it can happen that additional connections are formed between both the halves (so-called "synapses"). This then makes it possible for us to perform the exercise sequences more quickly. Studies of the brain have shown, for example, that by performing rhythmic exercise sequences (right half of the brain) the speech process can also be improved (left half of the brain). Thus, the stimulation of the functions of one half of the brain can also benefit the other.

- On the other hand, this pause offers a good opportunity to consider what has been learned and to prepare for what lies ahead. However, these pauses should not be longer than 10 minutes. In order to optimize learning, the first short pause should already take place after approximately 60 minutes of training.

- Shortly after completion of training, the material learned can still be recalled. A day later it is already almost impossible to remember all the details. The ability to remember also has to do with how much interest one has shown in following all of the training. Things, that are very interesting to someone, remain in their memory rather than the things that are not. For this reason, it is advisable that directly after the training the material that has been learned be reviewed (consolidated) and written down. It should be repeated the next day again and, if necessary, supplemented.

- Making notes helps the training to be processed mentally. One way is for the learner to read the description of the technique aloud and visualize the situation, similar to the way used in "shadowboxing." Another method is for the learner to imagine the whole situation. He sees himself in his thoughts – like in a film – in action and lives through the previous day's combinations. One can also record the notes on a cassette or CD and listen to them (for example, while commuting or at home). While one listens to the text, one should envisage the situation as colorfully as possible. So that one can note something especially well, it is advantageous to utilize as many senses as possible simultaneously. With this I mean not only the visual or acoustical senses, but above all also the sense of feeling. Things stay considerably better in my memory if I imagine the effect of a lever or a stranglehold intensively, rather than if I only hear the text. Exaggeration is also a method to remember what has been learned better.

- Positive thinking is necessary in order to be successful. If the trainee becomes negatively influenced before the lesson ("the other person is so big, so awfully strong, and also looks so dangerous..."), he won't often be successful because he has already given up in advance. If a human being positively motivates himself before a task (and that involves not only for sport), it will be considerably much easier for him to reach his goal.

- The setting of goals is also an important point. In order to be successful (and not only for sport) it makes sense to formulate short -, middle -, and long-term goals. These should however be realistic, that is, attainable. One can write the goals on a note and stick it (for example) to the bathroom mirror so that one is constantly reminded. A goal could be: "I will win the next championship."

- Autogenic training helps in the fulfillment of these goals. Here, the trainee always replaces a negative goal with a positive statement (a motto, for example) that he can accept in his subconscious. Wrong would be: "I have no fear." Better: "I can do it!" or: "I am brave." The reason lies in the fact that these formulations are automatically recalled in certain situations. For this area, as for that of mental training, there is an abundance of literature.

- For the purpose of realistic self-defense, from time to time the use of strike techniques should also be practiced in combination with knife attack techniques.

4 Competition Tips

- On the one hand, the mental training already mentioned is a good method for the preparation for the competition. Where possible, videos of the opponent should be obtained and his tactics and special techniques studied. Once the analysis has been completed, one can go through in one's mind how the opponent will use his techniques and what counter measures can be used to thwart him. On the other hand, one practices the feinting movements to induce the opponent to make a movement against which you can use one of your own special techniques.

- In order to get the right feeling, it is a good thing if you visit the place where the competition will take place at least one day before it does.

- If an analysis of the opponent cannot be done beforehand, it is also worthwhile to watch his fights at the tournament. The opponent can be divided roughly into two categories:
  - Passive
  - Active

  And then again into:
  - Long-range fighters
  - Contact fighters

  Your own trainer should know his fighter and advise him according to the capability of the opponent.

- For the competition fight it is not the final technique that is important. The important point is the position. The final technique springs out of the position. It is therefore important that one gets to master the positioning correctly.

- In the fight itself, the reserves of energy must be correctly apportioned. This factor is also influenced by tactical considerations.

- After the competition fight, the trainer must go through the actions that were carried out (where possible using a video analysis) so that the knowledge gained from it can be used to the best effect.

5 Transition from the Kicking Range to the Grappling Range

Basics: When bridging the gap, the position of your own head is important. It should be basically above the hip height of the opponent so that he cannot use a guillotine.

Bridging the gap can be started by using a feinting maneuver. D pulls himself up to his full height so that A has to bring his cover up. D then makes himself small in a rapid movement while at the same time moving forward quickly against A. Instead of using a feinting maneuver, in a fight where punches and kicks are allowed, a disturbing action (a punch or kick) can be employed in order to divert A's attention momentarily.

Another possibility is when A pulls back one of his extremities (arm or leg) after an attack. Simultaneously to the action of A pulling back D bridges the gap. D should always have in mind to keep his own cover well up (especially for the head). Particularly when executing a double leg takedown there is a danger of being hit by an uppercut, knee strike or similar.

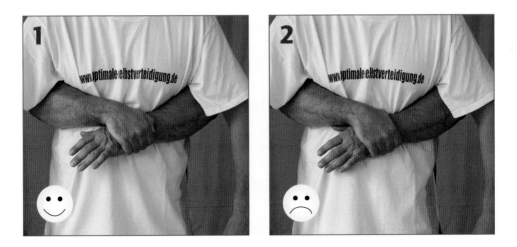

When gripping, D should make sure that all of his fingers lie together (Photo 1). If D grips his own wrist and has the thumb underneath with the other fingers on top (see Photo 2), then there is a danger that the arm muscles will quickly get tired and D will

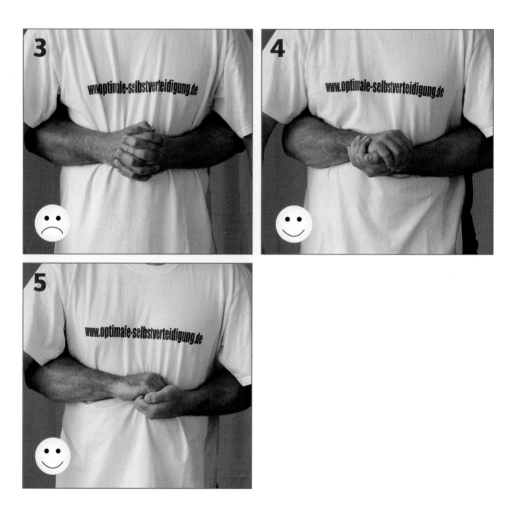

lose strength rapidly. Moreover, it will be difficult for D to be able to loosen this grip by using the reflexes. D should also not entwine his fingers together (see Photo 3), because A can get hold of them and easily lever them apart. It is best to grip over the left thumb with the fingers of the right hand (Photo 4) (or vice versa), or to lock the fingers underneath the fingers of the other hand (like two hooks) (see Photo 5).

The grip should be done just above waist height above the hips. This way, D can also pin A's arm. D must take care that where possible he pins A's elbow to his body in order to prevent A being able to use that arm for defense.

5.1 Start Position: A Stands with his Left Foot forwards and D Stands with his Right Foot forwards

1. A stands facing D. A is standing with his left foot forwards and D with his right foot forwards.
2. D carries out a feinting maneuver as if to grip A's head with both his hands. A brings his own hands upwards to cover his head.
3. Immediately, D places his right leg forwards (behind A) and pulls his left leg up to it (gliding movement). D moves close in towards A with good cover (his fists are protecting his own face) and wraps his arms round the body underneath A's arms.
4. D's head is lying on the upper left side of A's body at about rib height and the right leg is behind A.

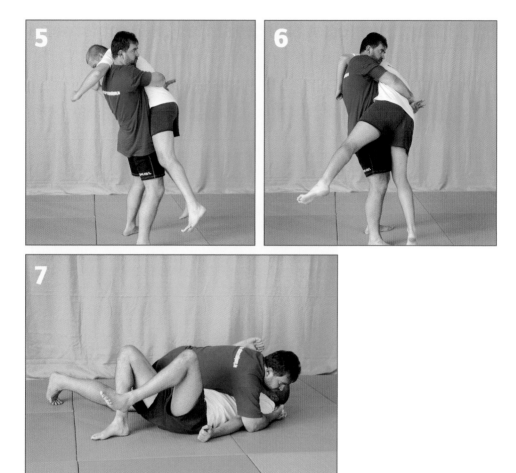

5. D stands up straight from the knees and lifts A up in a stemming movement and brings his right leg inwards so that is forced over horizontally...

6. ...and throws him down to the ground...

7. ...and pins him down with a crossover immobilizing lock (Side-mount, Cross position, Yoko Shio Gatame).

5.2 Start Position: Both A and D Stand with their Left Feet forwards

1. A stands facing D. Both are standing with their left feet forwards.
2. D carries out a feinting maneuver as if to grip A's head with both his hands. A brings his own hands upwards to cover his head.
3. D moves close in towards A with good cover by making a gliding movement starting with the right leg...
4. ...places his head on the upper left side of A's body and wraps his hands round A's lower legs...

5. ...lifts A with a double leg take-down...

6. ..and throws him down to the ground.

7.-8. D immediately pins A down with a crossover immobilizing lock (Cross position).

5.3   Start Position: Both A and D Stand with their Right Feet forwards

1. A stands facing D. Both are standing with their right feet forwards.
2. D carries out a feinting maneuver as if to grip A's head with both his hands. A brings his own hands upwards to cover his head.
3. D takes a lunging step forwards with his right leg and with good cover (his fists are protecting his head) places his head on the right-hand side of A's body.
4. As soon as D's head is beyond A's upper arm, he stretches up with the back of the head against A's upper arm so that A cannot wrap his arm round D's head. D is standing in front of A and grabs hold of him under the arms.

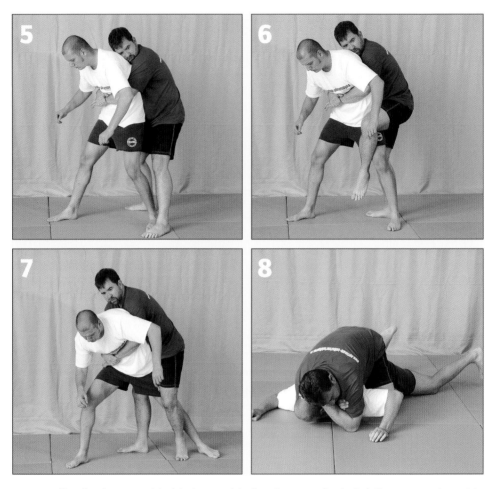

5. D slips further round behind A and jerks A's upper body briefly rearwards at hip height...

6. ...sweeps his left leg from the outside round A's left thigh...

7. ...pulls A's left leg rearwards so that A is forced to fall down.

8. D adopts the backmount position.

5.4 Start Position: A Stands with his Right Foot forwards and D Stands with his Left Foot forwards

1. A stands facing D. A stands with his right foot forwards and D stands with his left foot forwards.
2. D carries out a feinting maneuver as if to grip A's head with both his hands. A brings his own hands upwards to cover his head.
3. D takes a lunging step forwards with his right leg and with good cover (his fists are protecting his head) moves in close to A. As he does this he places his head beyond A's right upper arm.
4. As soon as D's head is beyond A's right upper arm, he stretches up with the back of the head against A's upper arm so that A cannot wrap his arm round D's head. D is standing in front of A and grabs hold of him under the arms...
5. ...he then slips round further until he is behind A.

6. He now places the sole of the left foot against the back of A's left heel...

7. ...lets the center of balance of his body drop towards the ground by bending the right knee and throws A to the ground...

8.-9. ...adopting the mount position.

6   Escrima (Rolling Arm)

This exercise (form of drill) can be compared to movements in Wing Tsun or Jeet Kune Do.

Description
Note: In this exercise, the neck is not gripped and the exercise should be carried out with slack actions.

1.   A stands facing D and each has his left arm thrust through underneath the opposite arm.
2.   Both try to get their right arms inside.

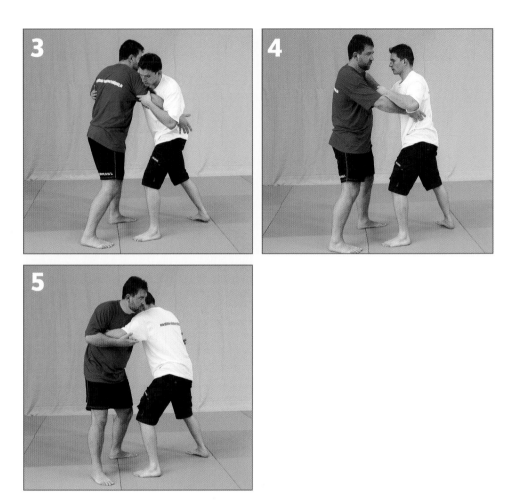

3.   When the arms have reached the inside, they are quite stretched out as if one wanted to grab round the hips.

4.   Both try now to get the left arms inside.

5.   When the arms have reached the inside, they are quite stretched out as if one wanted to grab round the hips.

And, now the exercise is done once again from the beginning.

6.1 Methods of Moving round to the Back

Over the Arm

1. Using an Escrima action, D grabs hold of A's diagonally opposed arm.
2. Once he has managed to get his arm inside and A's arm is just coming inside...
3. ...D grabs hold of the arm from underneath, pulls A forwards...
4. ...and gets round behind his back.

Underneath the Arm

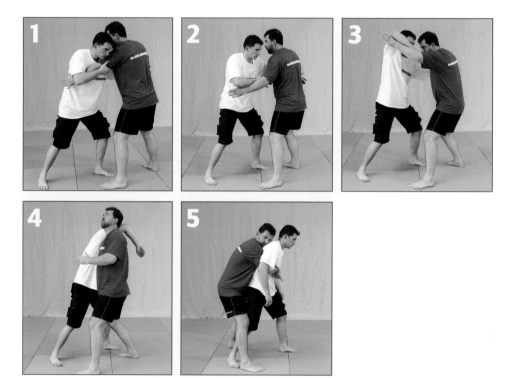

1. Using an Escrima action.
2. As A tries to bring his right arm inwards...
3. ...D lifts his left arm up...
4. ...ducks through under A's right arm and then stretches himself up straight away and pushes the back of his neck against A's right upper arm to prevent a guillotine action...
5. ...and gets round behind his back.

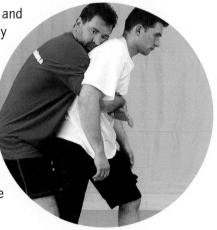

Note: This exercise serves to practice timing. In time one gets to learn the feeling when one can get round behind the back of the opponent.

Counter Technique: As soon as A tries to get behind D's back, D hollows his back and turns.

Follow-on Technique: If D cannot get round behind A's back, because he runs round following him, then D can execute a stop kick with the foot at A's knee and then get round behind his back.

Exercise

1. Both stand facing each other. Both are grasping the others opposite left hand...
2. ...and both are trying to get round behind the other's back.
3. The one who manages to do this first gets a point.

If this doesn't get a result then there are the following variations:

Variation 1:

D has to push A back over a particular line.
If D manages this he then gets the point (Photos 1 & 2).

Variation 2:

If D manages to get round behind A's back then he gets a point (Photos 1-3).

Note: For warm-ups this exercise has the advantage that it is a good exercise for the competition.

6.2 Follow-on Techniques from Escrima

1. Using an Escrima action, D gets round behind A's back.
2. D lifts A up (20 cms)...

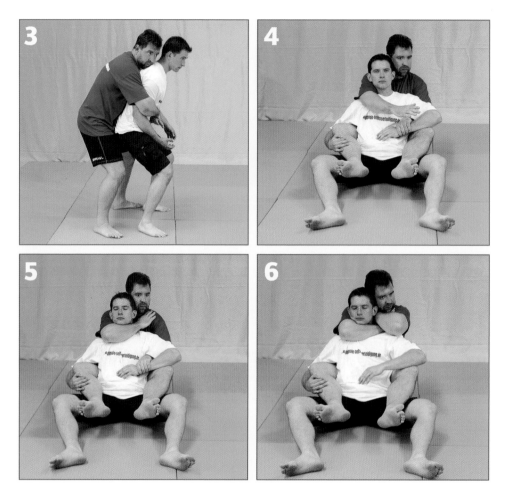

3.   ...and lets him fall down onto his feet so that A has to give at the knees.

4.   D falls backwards bringing A with him and pins A's thighs down using both of his feet (the feet are not crossed over)...

5.   ...and applies a Mata Leao (stranglehold with the lower arm) from behind. To do this D brings his right lower arm right round A's neck and lays his right hand on his own left shoulder.

6.   D pushes the left hand behind the nape of A's neck (with the palm pushing against the head) and obtains the strangling effect by tensing the upper arm and the upper back muscles (Mata Leao = lion killer).

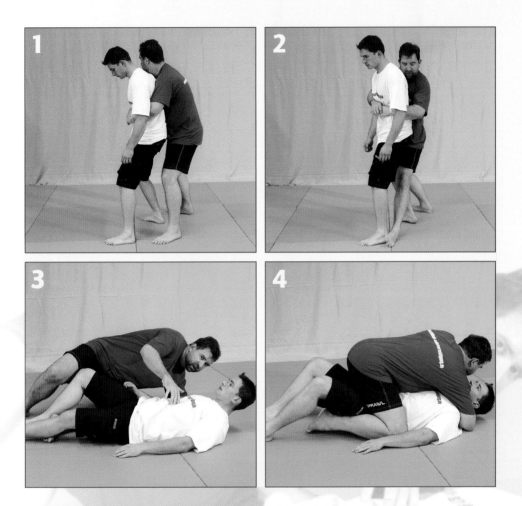

1. Using an Escrima action, D gets round behind A's back.
2. D places his left foot behind A's left heel...
3. ...and brings A down to the ground with a throw...
4. ...and then immediately gets into the mount position.

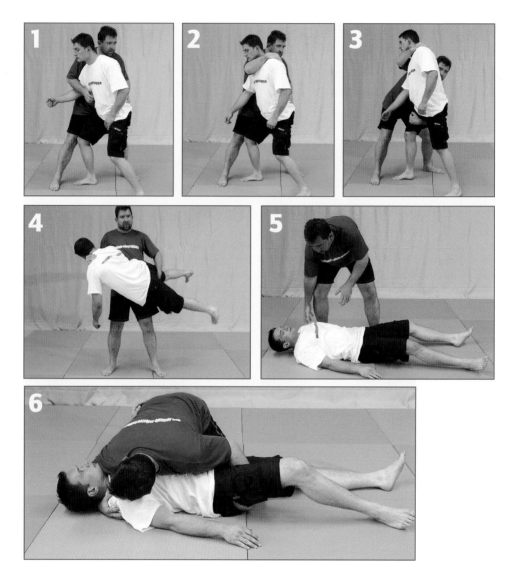

1.   Using an Escrima action, D gets alongside A on his right...
2.   ...brings his right arm round in front of A's neck...
3.   ...and with his left arm he reaches down and grabs hold of A's right thigh through from behind...
4.   ...lifts A up into a horizontal position (stretching the legs up and pushing the hips forward)...
5.   ...turns him over and brings him down onto the ground...
6.   ...where he immobilizes him in the cross position (Yoko Shio Gatame).

1. Just as D begins to bring his right arm into the inside...

2. ...he grabs the nape of A's neck with his right hand...

3. ...and leads the neck underneath and under the armpit of his left shoulder (his own hand is placed directly into the pit of the arm).

4. The left arm is brought from underneath round A's neck...

5. ...and the left hand grasps hold of D's own right wrist.

6. See detailed photo of the hold.

7. In this way a stranglehold (guillotine) is started using the arms. The legs are kept well together in order to protect the genital area as much as possible,

8. From this position, D could swing both his legs round A's hips and bring him down to the ground, immobilizing A in the guard position.

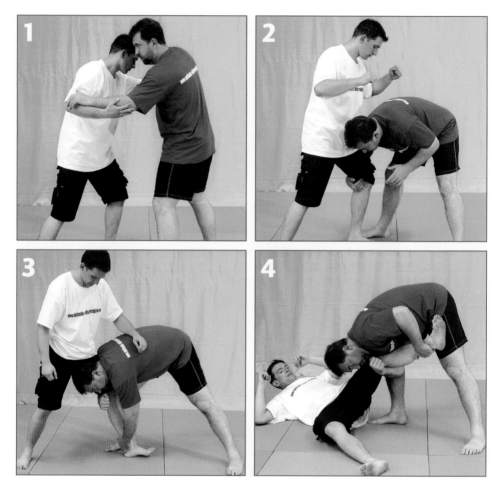

1. Just as D begins to bring his right arm into the inside, he grabs hold of A's left leg with his right hand...
2. ...brings his head to the inside of A's left thigh...
3. ...grabs hold of A's left lower leg with his left hand...
4. ...and brings A down to the ground with a single leg takedown.

1. Just as D has got his arm outside, he turns and executes a Sambo roll.

2. D is standing on A's left side and grabs round with his right arm to take hold of the nape of A's neck...

3. ...hooks his right leg into the hollow of A's right knee...

4. ...bows down forward and with his left arm grabs hold of the hollow of A's left knee round from the outside...

5. ...and then, lifting his left leg up to the rear, he does the Sambo roll.

6. D grabs hold of A's left thigh and slips along it...

7. ...executing a leg lock to immobilize A on the ground.

1. D's right arm is underneath A's left arm. D places his right hand on A's back.

2. D now also pushes the left hand through under A's right arm and thus has both arms under A's arms and round his back and he applies a grip like this under the arms.

3. D has his arms just above A's hips. With a pull of the arms and using his head to exert strong pressure against A's upper body he causes A to arch his back...

4. ...and then he walks forwards...

5. ...so that A is brought down to the ground.

7 Transition from Standing to the Ground (Take-downs)

7.1 Double Leg Take-down

Principles

- D takes hold of both legs.
- A is made to fall down.
- D must take care not to end up in A's guard.

Note: In a double leg take-down, in which D brings his legs past to the right and left (as done in Jiu-Jitsu) there is a danger that A can get D into the guard position. Following on from a successful throw/take-down, the thrower should always be the one who is dominant.

Execution – as practiced in Luta-Livre for example:

There are three possibilities.

No 1 (Press over and go round the outside)

1. D is covering his head...
2. ...and kneels down on the right, placing his left foot in front of A's right foot...

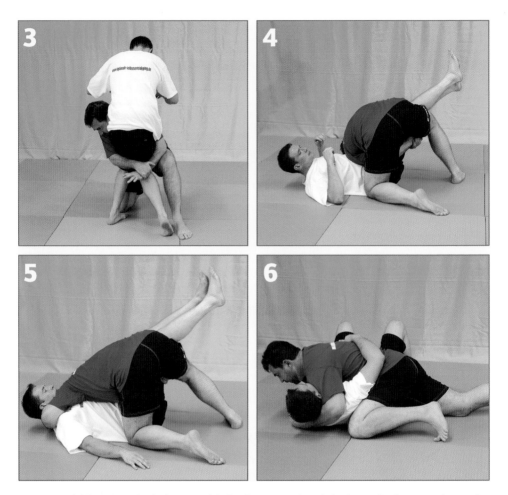

3.   ...grabbing round A's knees with both arms. The right knee is then at about the height of the left heel and the distance between the heel and the knee is only a few centimeters.

4.   D now presses hard forwards, goes round A and causes him to fall backwards. D grabs hold of the legs firmly, presses hard against A's upper body with the shoulders and lifts his hips well up while placing his right leg under A's legs that are still lifted up in the air.

5.   D only now loosens his grip and brings his left arm e.g., behind the nape of A's neck...

6.   ...he then lays his right arm over A's stomach and immobilizes A in the cross position (Yoko Shio Gatame).

No 2 (Using a minor roundhouse sweep)

1. D is covering his head...
2. ...and kneels down on the right, placing his left foot in front of A's right foot and grabs hold of A's knees with both arms.
3. Coming in from the outside, D places his left foot between A's legs.
4. D now presses firmly forwards and executes a kind of minor roundhouse sweep bringing A to fall over backwards. D grabs hold of the legs firmly, presses hard against A's upper body with the shoulders and lifts his hips well up.
5. D then turns round 180° while placing his right leg under A's legs, that are still held lifted up in the air.
6. D only now loosens his grip and brings his left arm e.g., behind the nape of A's neck...
7. ...he then lays his right arm over A's stomach and immobilizes A in the cross position (Yoko Shio Gatame).

No 3 (Using a Lift)

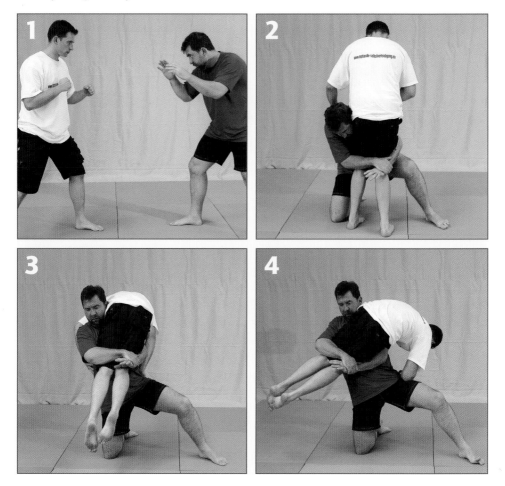

1. D is covering his head...
2. ...and then kneels down on his right knee and places his left foot in front of A's right foot and grabs round A's knees with both arms. The right knee is now level with the heel (A's) and the distance between the knee and the heel is only a few centimeters.
3. D lifts A up...
4. ...turns him into a horizontal position...

5. ...and makes him fall over backwards. D grabs hold of the legs firmly, pushing his shoulders hard against A's upper body and lifts his own hips right up.

6. D then turns round 180° while placing his right leg under A's legs, that are still held lifted up in the air.

7. D only now loosens his grip and brings his left arm e.g., behind the nape of A's neck...

8. ...he then lays his right arm over A's stomach and immobilizes A in the cross position (Yoko Shio Gatame).

Addendum: Should D also fall down during the takedown:

- D turns his body over its own axis once while holding onto A's legs firmly (Crocodile roll). After this D can carry on as usual.

Execution, as practiced for example in shootfighting:

If, for example, the attacker does a punch at the head, this is an opportunity to apply a double leg take-down.

Note: The double leg take-down is carried out to one side, because in a throw rearward, A could counter D with a scissor kick to the kidneys.

Structured Exercises

Step No 1

1. D is standing with his left foot forwards and first of all executes a gliding step forwards with the left (right) foot, so that his left foot is alongside A's left foot. He then drops down rapidly so that his right leg is touching the ground from the knee downwards. Make sure that the hips are square on to A (central line)
2. D's left shoulder is lying on A's left thigh. The upper body is upright and the hips are thrust forwards. The head – held on the left side of A's upper body - is not lowered so that A cannot press it down.
3. When D now brings his left knee down to the ground and the right comes up forward, A is lightly pushed towards the rear.

Training Tips

Practice the start alone, noting...

1. Duck down and glide forwards.
2. Right leg from the knee down is on the ground. Hips are square on to the attacker.
3. The left knee is placed on the ground. The right leg is immediately brought forward by bringing the knee up forwards, and the foot is placed on the ground.
4. D stands up and simulates the throw.

Repeat the sequence several times.

Step No 2

5. At the moment that D places his left knee on the ground he pulls A's left leg upwards and places his right leg between A's legs and props his knee up. His leg must not be placed out to the side otherwise A would hang from his leg and be able to prevent the throw. As the leg is lifted, A is tipped over to the side.

Step No 3

6. D now stands up and places his left leg outwards close to A's right leg and then presses with his left shoulder against A's upper body. It is important that D keeps a straight upper body, otherwise A could trap D in a frontal bear hug. The whole movement of shifting the weight comes from the legs. The upper body remains perpendicular. If D does not place his left leg alongside A's right leg, A can jump round D's hips and grab hold of him. D hooks his left knee round inside against A's right knee. D's left hand carries on holding the hollow at the back of A's right knee. The left foot is directly alongside A's right foot. D looks towards the left in the direction of the throw.

Step No 4

7. It is important that D's left foot is angled pointing 45° forward in the direction of the throw, because D will now move forward onto his left knee. Further, pressure is exerted with the left shoulder and the head against A's upper body. It should be noted that A's legs are brought past D's body properly during the throw, because otherwise D could injure himself on A's knee.

A falls down onto his back. D keeps both hands gripping the hollows at the back of A's knees and props his right leg up. A's right leg is lying over his right leg. As the throw was executed, A's legs came upwards so that it was possible for D to get a leg under A's legs. D's main weight is lying on A's upper body, because D is pressing his left shoulder hard against it.

After this a position is taken up so that D is very close to A i.e., his knees are close to him. As an immobilizing action the following example could be used:

Push the left arm through underneath the nape of A's neck and apply pressure on the left side of the neck with the left upper arm in the direction of A's head and take hold of your own left arm with the right hand. The right leg is stretched out to the rear.

Situation: D could not get close enough between A's legs and has no proper control over A's legs and he gets out free to the rear.

1. Now, D doesn't bring his right leg between A's legs, but brings it from the outside round the left leg so that the hollow of his own knee is close behind A's heel.
2. D's body is lying close alongside A's left leg.
3. D applies pressure forwards and brings A down to the ground in a fall backwards. Now D can bring his right leg underneath A's left leg and angle the leg to create a Sangaku (Figure Four, Triangle). D presses against A's right knee with his hips and in the other direction with his legs, A's leg is placed in a lock.

7.2 Special Leg Grip - Single Leg Take-down (Kuiki-kata-ashi-dori)

The single leg take-down is shown to the beginner in such a way that the opponent's legs are brought past one's own legs. The advanced student can bring the opponent's leg between his own legs.

1. D is standing in front of A and pulls A's left arm down with both hands. A is standing with his left leg forwards.

2. A tries to loosen the grip being applied by D by pulling in the opposite direction. D uses the momentum given by A and lets the arm go, drops down onto his left knee and props his right leg forwards while ensuring good cover of his head as he does this. The head is placed on the inside of the left thigh and with his right arm then grabs hold of the left leg at the height of about the hollow of the knee. With his left hand he grabs hold of the area just above the heel on the same leg.

3. He now pulls with both arms and applies pressure downwards with the shoulders while pressing with the head against the inside of the thigh...

4.   ...so that A falls over backwards. D presses firmly against A's upper body with his shoulders and at the same time lifts his hips well up rapidly...

5.   ...and then turns round 180°. D brings his right arm round behind the nape of A's neck, lays his right arm over A's stomach and immobilizes A in the cross position (Yoko Shio Gatame).

1.   D is standing in front of A. Both of D's hands are round A's neck and are pulling it down. A is standing with his left leg forwards.

2.   A is pulling his head up against the hands as hard as he can. D uses the momentum given by A and lets the head go...

3.   ...drops down onto his left knee and props his right leg forwards behind A's left leg. D's left knee is directly alongside A's left leg. D's right foot is about where A's right foot is placed. The head is placed on the inside of A's left leg and with his left arm then grabs hold of A's left leg.

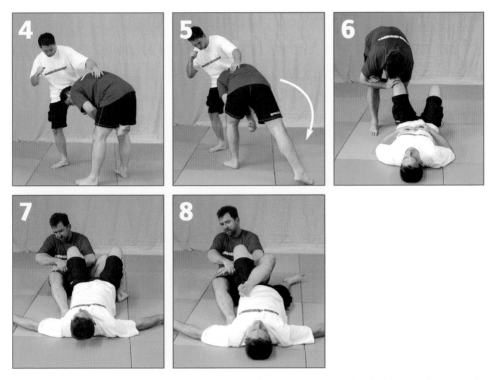

4. D slowly stands up by stretching his left leg. D's upper body is very close to A's left thigh.

5. D does a step turn through 90° to the rear with his right leg and at the same time pushes against A's thigh with his upper body...

6. ...so that A falls over backwards. A's leg is directly between D's legs.

7. D gets down close alongside A's left leg. A's left foot is underneath D's bottom. D pulls back firmly against the calf of A's left leg.

8. D prevents A standing up by placing his left foot over A's left thigh.

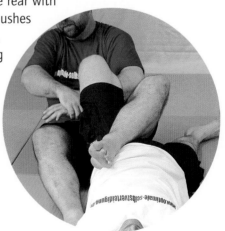

7.3 Correct Changeover between the Double Leg Take-down and the Single Leg Take-down (Kuiki-kata-ashi-dori) (Double and Single Leg Take-down)

1. D tries to execute a double leg take-down on A.
2. A places his right leg to the rear so that D does not manage to grab round the legs.
3. D brings his left arm onto the inside, grabs hold of A's left leg with his left hand and brings his head round inwards.

Note: If the head is kept outwards during the single leg take-down, A can easily block by applying pressure with the thigh outwards. If the head is brought inwards, D can push round into the throwing position more successfully.

4. D pushes forwards and brings his leg outwards past his own left leg and makes him fall over backwards. D grabs hold of the legs firmly, pushes hard against A's upper body with his shoulders and lifts his hips up well.

5. Then D turns round 180°, places his right leg underneath A's legs that are being still held lifted up.

6. D only now lets go of the grip and brings his left (for example) arm round behind the nape of A's neck...

7. ...lays his right arm over A's stomach and immobilizes A in the cross position (Yoko Shio Gatame).

Note: This changeover can be taught as a sequence of actions. If, for example, a student blocks a double leg take-down when practicing, this technique can be brought in and the sequence shown.

7.4   Counter Moves against the Double Leg Take-down

Always use the Kanga blocking action (counter against a double leg take-down) by carrying out a pushing movement through under the opponent's shoulders with the arms. Just stopping the opponent using the lower arms against the shoulders will do nothing for Grappling – it is even a disadvantage.

- Preventing the action by dodging and using the Kanga block

1. A starts to execute a double leg takedown.
2. D dodges back on one leg, pushes both arms or just only one arm (Mea) through underneath A's arms and prevents the double leg takedown being carried out. In the Mea-Kanga, one arm is pushed up from underneath and the other down over or down under the opponent's arm.
3. D brings his arm round A's neck on the side where his head is...
4. ...and, with the other hand he grabs hold of his own hand and pulls this upwards. D pushes his hips forwards hard and stands upright.

1. A tries to do a double leg take-down.

2. D dodges back on one leg, pushes both arms, or just only one arm, (Mea) through underneath A's arms and prevents the double leg take-down being carried out. In the Mea-Kanga, one arm is pushed up from underneath and the other down over or down under the opponent's arm.

3. D jumps backwards with open legs (sprowl).

4. D can now get A down on the ground (but doesn't have to!).

5. When doing this D has his head on A's back...

6. ...and in this position, he can carry out a stranglehold using the lower arms (Guillotine).

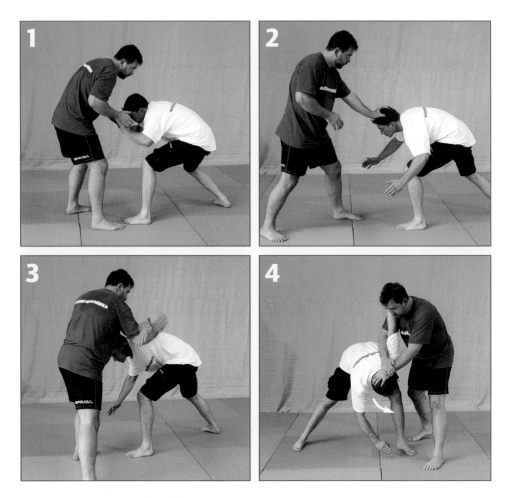

1. A starts a double leg take-down.
2. D pulls his left leg to the rear and stops A by thrusting his left hand against A's head. A has his left leg forward and D also has his left leg forward.
3. D reaches through under A's left arm with his right arm...
4. ...and lays his right hand over his left hand that is held on top of A's head...

5. ...does a 90° turn to the rear and brings A down to the ground.
6. A's left arm is held firmly just above A's left elbow by his right arm. This controlling action and the pull is very important, because if balance is lost using this grip it can be easily regained. The secret is the action of pulling on A's upper arm. D kneels down with his right knee on A's right upper arm to pin it down. If A's right upper arm is stretched out to the rear, this presents no problem. In such a case, D simply kneels down on the ground directly alongside A.
7. The left foot is placed close to A's upper body.
8. D turns clockwise to the left and applies a sideways stretching lock (knees together, pulling A's left arm down towards the mat so that his little finger is pointing down towards the mat.

8 Further Transitions from Standing to the Ground (Take-downs)

1. A and D are standing with their left feet forward. A tries to get hold of D's neck with his right hand.
2. D turns A's right arm inwards with his left hand...
3. ...swings his right arm through under A's left arm and puts it round A's neck. The right arm is lying on A's back and is pointing towards the ground at 45°.
4. D now brings his left fist onto A's right-hand side at about kidney height (both of D's fists are pointing at each other). D presses into A's back firmly so that A has to push his hips forward and bend over backwards.

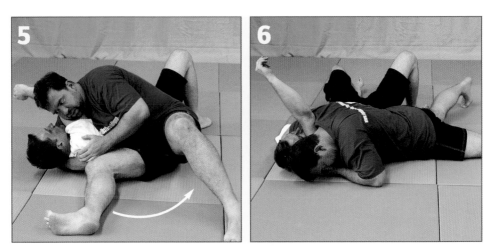

5. D brings A down to the ground and immobilizes A with a side mount lock (Kesa Gatame).
6. D lays alongside A's right-hand side and takes hold of his left hand with his other hand and applies a stranglehold.

1. A and D are standing with their left feet forward. A gets hold of D's neck with his right hand.

2. D moves forward so that his own head is positioned on the center of A's chest and grabs round A's upper body with both arms...

3. ...hooks his right foot round A's left leg...

4. ...then hooks his left foot round A's right leg...

5. ...and makes A fall down backwards. D goes into the mount position. In this situation D can now apply for example a stranglehold.

1. A is standing behind D and has grabbed round D under the arms.
2. D throws his weight forwards to make it more difficult for A to throw him backwards onto his neck (suplex).
3. D places the right arm round from the outside over A's right elbow and pins A's arm to his body. D places his the right leg outwards and bending...

4. ...turns in and using an outward reaping throw brings A down to the ground.
5. D turns round further and gets himself into the cross position (side mount).

9 Ground Techniques

9.1 Eight Steps to Becoming a Successful Ground Fighter

The student should first of all gain an understanding of the techniques and then go on to practice the various attributes such as agility, strength and speed. After having learned these it is a good idea to develop a strategy for the competition.

Splitting down the various elements of the training plan it is best to approach it in the following manner:

Step 1:
The student is placed in a situation where he has to break free from the various holds. He has to be able to recognize where the attacker will place his weight and ascertain where there is room to be able to change his position.

Step 2:
Then the student learns to be able to hold and control his position and adapt his own position to that of the attacker's movements. For this the student has to learn how to use his own weight to the best advantage and stay close to the opponent.

Step 3:
In this step, the exercises are complemented by using stranglehold and lever techniques, aimed at making the opponent submit.

Step 4:
After learning the basics the physical attributes (agility, strength and speed) can be practiced.

Step 5:
In Step 5, the student is taught counter measures and follow-on techniques i.e., he will now learn techniques that can be used against those techniques started by the opponent. He will also learn techniques that can be used if the opponent prevents him using one of his techniques.

Step 6:
Here, the student learns counter measures against strangleholds and lever techniques.

Step 7:
Everything that has been learned must now be practiced on the weaker side of the body.

Step 8:
Now go on to fight, fight and keep on fighting.

9.2 The Principles of Groundwork

Gaining Room
In Step 1, the student learns to break free from the various positions. This means he has to gain room to be able to prepare to break free in the best way he can. In Step 2, it is important to be able to maintain that position. For this the opponent must not be given any opportunity to be able to break free.

Weight
One has to be able to sense where the opponent is placing his weight or at least where he is leaving a hole that can be exploited by an escape action. When you are controlling and holding a position, you must be able to use your weight to the best advantage to make it difficult for the opponent. Being able to adjust your weight when the opponent moves his weight is also an important factor.

Timing
Timing is a very important factor in the fight. Dependent on the competition rules (fights with no time limit) it is important to divide your energy up sensibly. The experienced fighter is able to come up with the optimum mixture of power periods and passive actions. When a muscle is fully tensed, after a few seconds the initial energy reserves – the phosphates and then the glycogens – have been used up. These reserves can be refreshed, which however takes time and cannot be as good as before the fight began.

After using the glycogens, then the fat reserves come into play. If an athlete is fighting in the aerobic phase then he is able to recoup his energy by burning up fats. These reserves permit the fighter to last a long time.

An indicator for the layman to be able to ascertain that he is in this state, is when he is able still to speak three sentences one after the other. If you don't have enough breath to be able to do this, then you are in the anaerobic state i.e., energy production comes from the phosphates and glycogens. The phosphates are already present inside the muscles and permit the muscles to contract. The glycogens are also, in part, in the muscle and in the liver.

Lactates (lactic acid) are produced during the anaerobic phase. Too many lactates overacidify the body and the muscles can cramp up and movements steered by the brain are not coordinated. The heart muscle breaks down the lactates into the body. Therefore, in such a state the fighter should not sit down during the breaks, but remain standing, moving about from one foot to the other on the spot so that the blood is pumped well to the heart. This is called *active recuperation*.

Characteristics

An experienced fighter not only possesses great strength, stamina, good coordination, agility and speed but also he has a good sensitivity. He must be able to have a good feel for what the opponent has in mind and react accordingly in good time.

9.3   Bridging the Gap when the Opponent is Lying on the Ground in Front of You

1.   A is lying on his back on the ground in front of D. His legs are aimed in D's direction.
2.   D grabs hold of the outsides of both of A's knees with both hands and tries to press them together. A reacts reflexively and applies an opposite pressure, bringing his legs outwards.

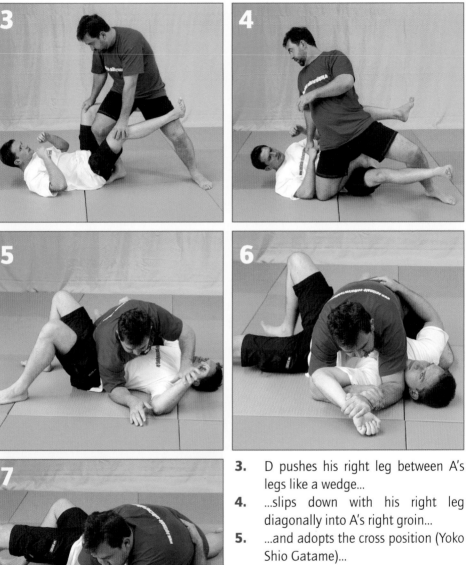

3. D pushes his right leg between A's legs like a wedge...
4. ...slips down with his right leg diagonally into A's right groin...
5. ...and adopts the cross position (Yoko Shio Gatame)...
6. ...grabs hold of A's left wrist with his left hand and then pushes his right arm underneath A's left arm and grabs hold of his own left wrist. D lifts the wrists up...

7. ...pulls the left elbow to A's left hip and lifts A's left elbow up with the right arm so that the bent arm lock (Francesa, Ude Garami) is effective. A's left hand is kept firmly on the ground.

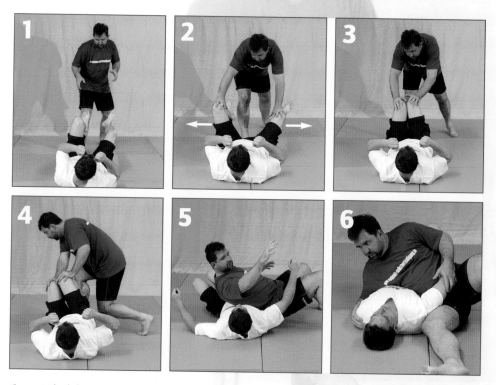

1. A is lying on his back on the ground in front of D. His legs are aimed in D's direction.

2. D grabs hold of the insides of both of A's knees with both hands and tries to press them apart.

3. A reacts reflexively and presses his knees together.

4. D rolls over onto...

5. ...A's right side...

6. ...and gets into a scarf hold (Kesa Gatame)...

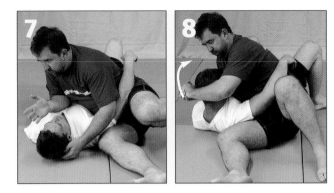

7. ...presses his right elbow into A's breastbone...

8. ...and grabs hold of A's head with his left hand. His right hand grips hold of his own left hand. With pressure applied by the elbow and by pulling the head forward, a neck lock is performed.

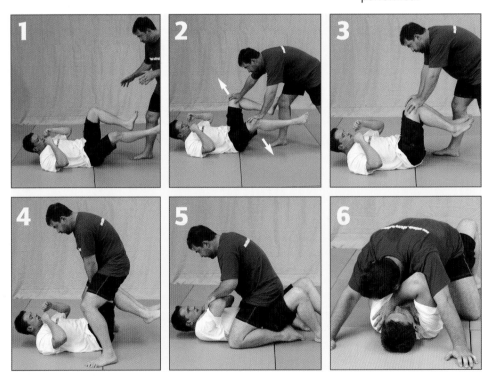

1. A is lying on his back on the ground in front of D. His legs are aimed in D's direction.

2. D grabs hold of the insides of both of A's knees with both hands and tries to press them outwards.

3. A reacts reflexively and presses his knees together.
4. D slides over A's thigh...
5. ...onto his upper body and adopts the mounted position. A protects his neck by placing both arms crossed in front of it.
6. D puts his left shoulder up against A's right upper arm and places his hands to the left and right on the ground to the side of A's body.
7. D presses A's right arm onto A's left side with his left shoulder...
8. ...and grabs hold of A's right wrist with the right hand on the outside...
9. ...brings his own head onto A's right upper arm...
10. ...pushes his right arm under A's neck...
11. ...and grabs hold of his own right hand with his left hand. D lies down directly alongside the right-hand side of A's body, brings his face to look at the ground and places his left leg out to the left as a support. D works the fingers of his right hand bit by bit along the ground to the left until they can go no further. He then grabs hold of the fingers of the right hand with the fingers of the left hand and applies a stranglehold.

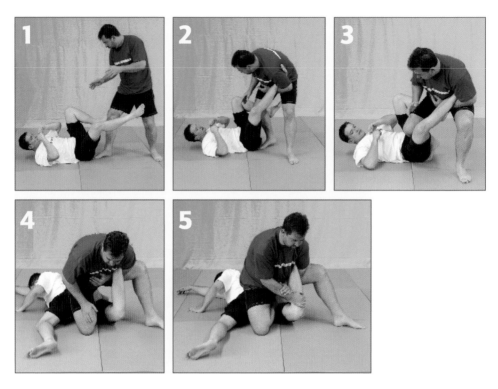

1. A is lying on the ground on his back in front of D, who is standing at A's feet. D is standing with his right leg forward so that he can get it between A's legs like a wedge. D's right foot is almost underneath A's right thigh.

2. D grabs down and up round A's right thigh and places his left hand on his own chest.

3. When D does not manage to drop down over A's groin when kneeling down, but comes more into the direction of the knee...

4. ...D turns round further to the left and brings A more into a stomach down position (A's foot stays during this underneath D's left armpit). The left leg is stretched out to the left and propped up.

5. D places his right hand on A's shinbone and locks the leg by grabbing hold of his own right wrist with his left hand and pushing the hips well forward. In this way the sole of A's foot is locked.

Note: Execute the technique slowly and in small steps, because the sinews are extremely sensitive to the strains.

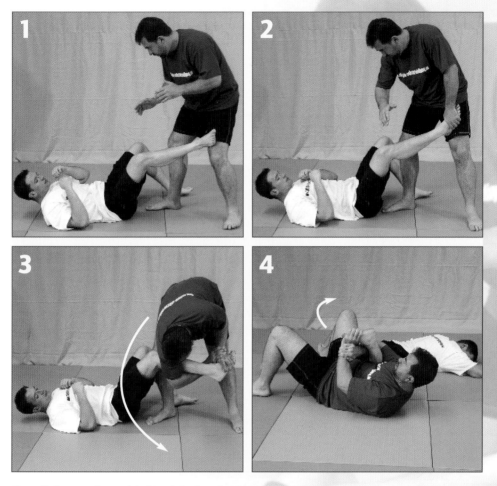

1. D is standing with his right leg forward in order to be able to get it between A's legs like a wedge. A presses his right foot against D's left thigh.
2. D grabs hold of A's right foot with his left hand. The fingers are pointing towards the ground...
3. ...grasps over A's right lower leg with his right hand and takes hold of his own left wrist (locking action).
4. D does a forward roll over his right shoulder. D thus forces A over to lie in the stomach position. D applies a locking action so that A has to submit.

9.4 The Guard Position

The guard position (Guarda) is divided into the following:

1. Full Guard
   • Closed guard (with legs crossed over)
   • Open guard (legs open)

2. Half (Mea) guard (the attacker has, for example, a grip on one of the defender's legs)

For the defender there are two situations:

• The defender is lying on his back and has got the attacker in the guard.
• The defender is in the guard.

Note: If A has D in the guard, then he has control over D's body and, for example, can take actions using his arms. However, if D is between A's legs and D's arms are in front of A's legs the situation is more open, because D's arms are still on his sides. The limit is when they are at about the height of A's genital area. If D gets any higher than this with his arms then there is a danger that A can get hold of the arm and place a lock on it. Doing this, D practically surrenders his arms up to A to act with. The individual distances for these actions are described in the following.

Distance 1:
D is lying down on his back and is holding A down close to him. In this position, D perhaps has an advantage, because he can carry out more techniques than A. However, generally speaking the situation is about equal.

Distance 2:

D is lying on his back and A is kneeling upright between D's legs. In this position A has an advantage, because he can use more energy in his strikes than D. This is a position where A more or less is safe and could consider escaping himself from the guard position. If D opens his legs he is in danger of A carrying out a foot lock on him.

Distance 3:

A has managed to free himself from the guard position and is in front of D's feet. At this distance D can kick A. There are not many possibilities for A.

Distance 4:

A has managed to free himself from the guard position and has stood up. This position is like the first one and is seemingly equal.

If D wishes to attack from this position, it is advisable not to lie with the upper body touching the ground, but at least to get onto one side and lift up slightly. Just to defend he can keep his upper body still on the ground.

Lead-up Exercise

1. D is kneeling in front of A between his legs.
2. D now tries to get past A's legs and get into a different position (e.g., side position or mount position). All this should be carried out playfully.

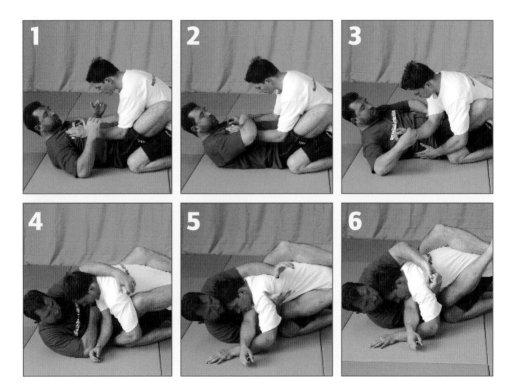

Control of the Arms

1. D has hold of A in the guard position. A lays both of his arms on D's chest.
2. D grabs hold of A's right wrist with his right hand and puts his left hand round behind A's right elbow.
3. By pulling to the right D brings A's right arm over to the right.
4. D lifts up his upper body and he takes hold of A's left latissimus with his left hand over his back.
5. The right hand pushes through underneath both arms so that D's right arm pins the right lower arm against A's body.
6. Then, D hooks his hands together behind A's back.

1. D has hold of A in the guard position. A lays both of his arms on D's chest.
2. D pushes his left arm through on the inside past through the inside of A's right upper arm and brings it round A's upper arm...
3. ...pulls the upper arm straight and brings the outstretched arm onto the left side of the neck and applies an arm lock.

Note: If the arm lock cannot be applied, because A angles his arm, D can still keep control of A's arm with this technique so that A is limited in his movement.

Final Techniques from the Guard Position

Note: First of all an escape action must be completed. Final techniques from the guard position are extremely difficult to perform.

Full Guard: D has A in the Guard Position with Both Legs Clamped round his Back

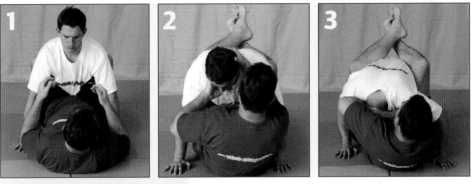

1. D has hold of A in the guard position. A is lifting his head up.
2. D takes hold of A's neck/under the chin (the palm of the hand is pointing towards the ceiling) with the left hand and his right hand is holding the nape of A's neck..
3. D pulls the head to the left underneath his left armpit.
4. D brings his left arm bit by bit to the right and with his right hand grabs hold of his own left arm and pulls it upwards. D keeps the guard applied and lays his head on A's back (don't drop the body back). If D drops his body back this leaves a space between D's chest and A's neck (the efficiency of the technique is only 95%). If D bends forward, the space is closed.

1. D has hold of A in the guard position. D takes hold of and pushes A's biceps with his left hand so that A is prevented from being able to strike with the arm.

2. D has released his clamped legs in the guard position a little. D pushes A's right arm inwards to the right and pushes his hips to the left underneath A...

3. ...places his left arm round A's back and takes hold of A's shoulder.

4. D's head is lying (closely) behind A's shoulder on the right hand side of the back of A's head. D's left leg is lying over the base of A's back. It is important that D controls A's shoulder/arm with his head, otherwise A can pull his right arm out and grab round D's head.

5. D now frees himself from underneath A and climbs up onto his back. D's left arm is under A's neck and right lower arm.

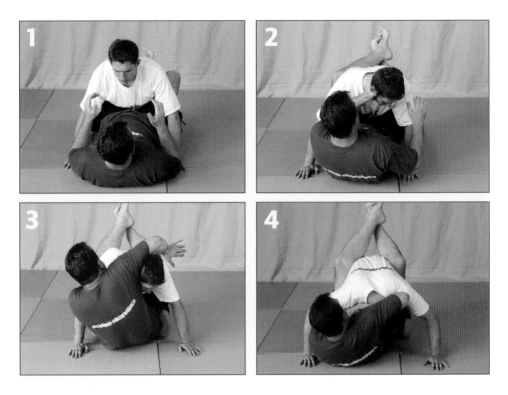

1. D has hold of A in the guard position and A is lifting his upper body up a little at about 45°.
2. D lifts his upper body upwards and using his left hand he pushes A's head to D's right side with his left hand...
3. ...swings his right arm down round the left hand side of A's neck...
4. ...brings his arm further round A's neck and grabs hold of his own right hand with his left hand and pulls himself backwards and stretches himself out executing a guillotine stranglehold technique. A's head is held on D's right hand side under his armpit. The left arm is pulling the neck in the direction of D's left shoulder.

1. D grabs hold of A's right wrist with the left hand.
2. Then D grabs hold (diagonally) of A's right arm close to the right elbow...
3. ...pulls the right arm inwards to the right and holds it firmly. D pulls his legs up so that A's upper body is brought forward and grabs hold of A's neck with his left hand and pulls A's head downwards...
4. ..."rolls" the left hand over A's head or directly grabs hold diagonally of the left-hand side of A's face whereby the palm of the left hand is lying on the left hand side of A's face.
5. D thrusts the head hard to the left.
6. D swings his left leg over A's head...

7. ...and places it stretched out onto the left hand side of A's neck...

8. ...and then wraps it round the head so that A's neck is in the hollow at the back of D's knee. He then places his right leg across A's back close to A's upper arm. He pulls his feet together and presses the heels towards the ground pressing his knees together and pushing his hips forward.

9. He then grabs round A's left leg with his right hand in order to make the arm lock more firm.

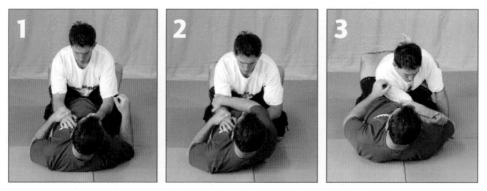

1. D has hold of A in the guard position and A is lifting his upper body up a little at about 45°. A has laid his arms on D's chest. D is grabbing hold of the right wrist with his left hand...

2. ...and reaches diagonally over his own chest and places his right hand on the outside over and behind A's right elbow.

3. D pulls A's right arm diagonally back over to the right hand side of his body...

4. ...and brings his hips outwards to the left...

5. ...swings his left leg up over A's neck and squeezes it in the hollow at the back of his knee, stretches his hips and makes A fall over this way. While carrying out the technique D is constantly keeping a controlling hold of A's right arm.

6. Where possible, D pushes his feet under A's left upper arm so that A cannot grab hold of the toes. D presses his knees together and lifts his hips up (his bottom is close to the right hand side of A's upper body so that A cannot turn over on to his left side thus making the leverage unworkable)...

7. ...and pulls the stretched out right arm downwards, or better still, pulls it over his right groin. When doing this A's little finger must point in the direction of the ground. This results in effecting a crossways stretched arm lock (Juji Gatame).

Note: Instead of pinning the outstretched right arm against the upper body with the hands, it is more effective to pin the outstretched arm to the body by using both arms. This way you can also use the strength of the body as well as the arms.

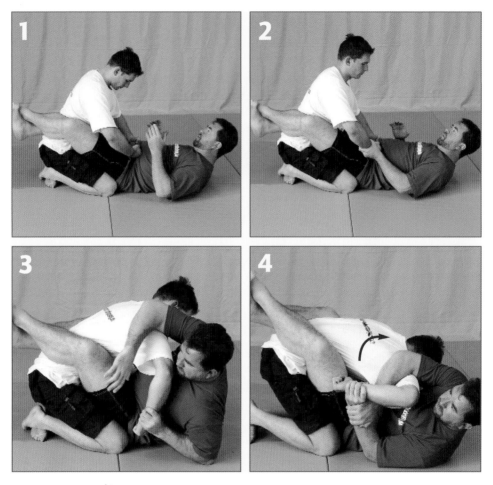

1.   D has hold of A in the guard position. D's head is raised up. A is pushing his fists into D's groin and **makes the mistake of having his right elbow jutting outwards**.

2.   D grabs hold of A's right wrist with his (parallel opposite) left hand...

3.   ...and lifts his upper body upwards to the left...

4.   ...grabbing hold of his own left wrist over A's right arm and lies back down again. As a result the left upper arm is on the ground alongside his body. In this position it takes a lot of strength and effort to effect a bent arm lock (Americano, Kimura, Ude Garami).

5. D opens his guard, but continues to immobilize A's upper body with his left leg and pushes his hips out to the left (D is practically lying on his side in this position). It is also possible to carry out this technique with a closed guard. This would make it safer but more difficult to do.

6. In this position D presses A's right hand in the direction of A's right shoulder using his left hand thus permitting a bent arm lock (Americano, Kimura, Ude Garami) to be applied fully.

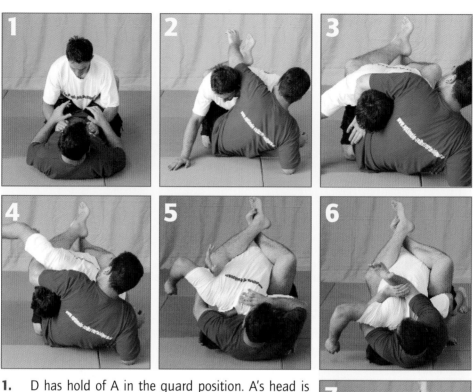

1. D has hold of A in the guard position. A's head is lifted up.
2. D lifts his upper body up forwards 45° to the right...
3. ...and grips round over A's head with his left arm...
4. ...pushing his left hand through under A's right armpit...
5. ...and places his right hand on A's shoulder from behind and pushes it downward.
   Note: The action of pushing down the shoulder moves the armpit from the horizontal into a position upwards to the left (as from D's aspect).
6. D bends his left arm inwards and lays his left hand on his own right upper arm.
7. Depending on how strong A is, D can place his left hand round his right elbow and place his right hand on his own head. Instead of placing it on the head, D can place his right hand on A's outstretched arm. D ends the combination with the crucifix technique.

Note: Both of the last two techniques can be used to good effect in the following combination.

1. D has hold of A in the guard position. A makes the mistake of holding his left elbow outwards.
2. D tries to apply a bent arm lock (Americano, Kimura).
3. A blocks and lifts himself up.
4. D grabs round the head and applies a guillotine.

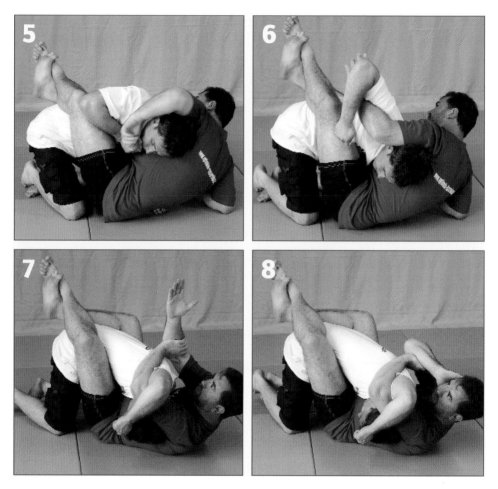

5. A blocks by bringing his hand between himself and D's arm.
6. D pushes his left arm through underneath A's right arm...
7. ...places the left hand on his own right lower arm...
8. ...and ends the combination with the crucifix technique.

1. D has hold of A in the guard position. A is strangling D with both hands.
2. In order to exercise more pressure on the neck, A jumps up onto both feet and tries to increase the stranglehold.
3. D pushes his hips upwards with a quick strong movement so that A loses his grip on the neck...
4. ...and D sweeps A's arms to the right with his left hand...

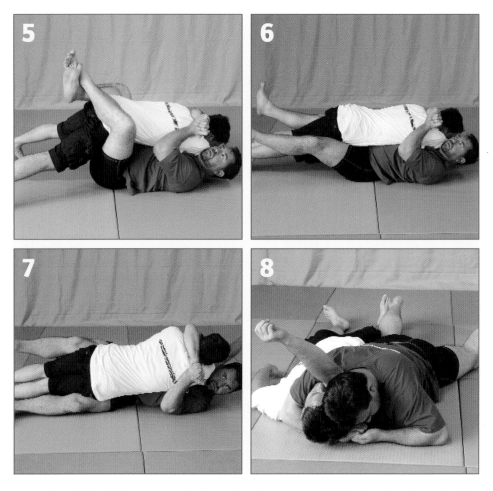

5. ...leads the right arm round A's neck and presses with the head against A's right upper arm...
6. ...stretches out both of his legs and clamps A's between them...
7. ...then turns over to the left...
8. ...so that A is on his back. D immediately positions himself alongside the right side of A's body, places his left leg out sideways in order to lie in a more stable position and effects a stranglehold (strangling using his own lower arm).

Full Guard: The Legs are Open

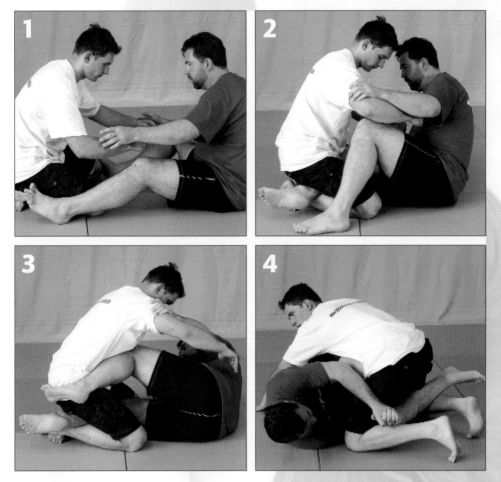

1. D is sitting with his legs open facing A, who is kneeling in front of D.
2. D's left foot is next to A's right knee and his right foot is next to A's left knee. D pushes his right leg between A's legs underneath the right thigh and lies onto his right side. He then places his left knee against A's lower ribcage (on A's right hand side), in order to maintain and control proper distance. D's feet are crossed over at about the height of A's right thigh (half guard, Mea Guard).
3. D grabs round A's left knee with both arms.
4. This shows the position from the other side.
5. D swings his right leg round from the outside over A's left thigh...

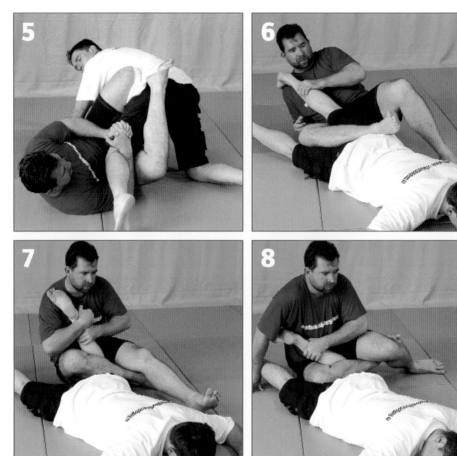

6. ...turns A over clockwise onto his stomach, pushing A backwards with the left leg. A's left foot is next to the right hand side of D's neck.

7. D swings the left leg over his own right instep (Sangaku, Figure Four, Triangle)...

8-9. ...and ends the combination with a leg lock by lifting up his hips.

1. A has managed to free himself from the guard and place his left leg out to one side.

2. If D doesn't react, A can hit D. As quickly as possible, D places his right leg into A's groin and places his knee close against A's shoulder.

3. If A now also places his right leg out and tries to stand up. D must do the same as before with his right leg.

4. From this position D stretches out jerking backwards so that D's head and upper body are no longer in striking range by A. D's genital area, however, is vulnerable so D must not stay long in this position.

5. D thrusts A backwards with the full force of his legs and then stands up immediately.

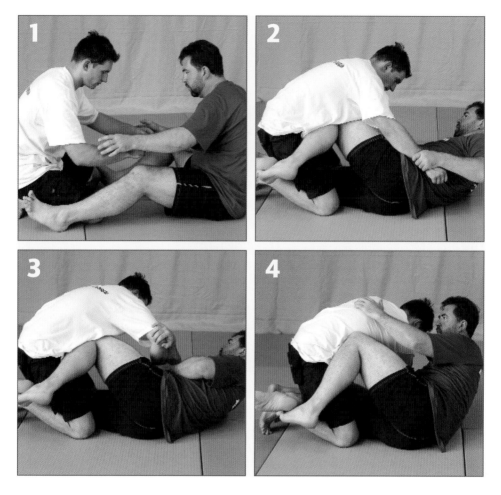

1. D is lying on the right side of his body in front of A and has his right leg between A's legs and his left knee is in front of A's upper body to maintain the proper distance. His feet are crossed over about the height of A's right thigh.
2. D grabs hold of A's right wrist with his left hand...
3. ...and grabs hold behind A's right elbow with the right hand and pulls A's right arm down alongside the right hand side of his body.
4. D's upper body is lifted up...

5. ...and is positioned behind the right rear hand side of A's back.
6. D now brings his upper body round directly behind A's back.
7. D then thrusts through underneath past the armpit of A's left lower arm with his left arm. D pushes his left leg round A's left leg and between his legs.
8. D pulls A's left arm inwards so that A loses his balance.

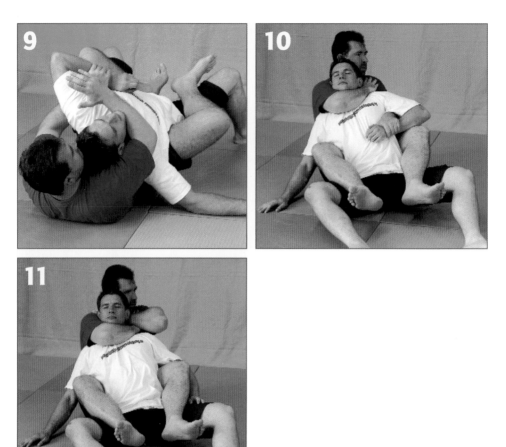

9. D places his right lower arm underneath A's throat and at the same time places his right hand behind A's left shoulder. D turns over counterclockwise and keeps hold of A who is lying between his legs.

10. D applies a stranglehold on A with his right lower arm. D supports the technique by stretching back and pulling his right arm downwards to the right. This results in the knuckle of the right hand being placed directly next to the larynx. The feet are not crossed over so that A cannot lay his leg over the feet and apply a foot lever as a counter measure. D's left arm keeps hold of A's left wrist throughout.

11. In this position, D can now let go of the left wrist and push his left hand against the rear of A's head (with the back of the hand against the head). D can now apply the stranglehold using the lower arm (lion-tamer, Mata Leao).

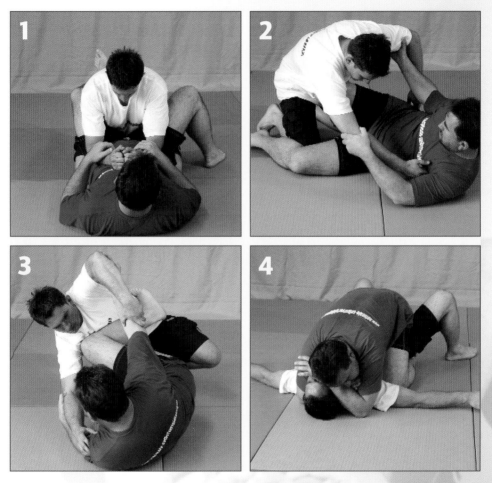

1. D is holding A in the guard position. D opens his guard...
2. ...and brings his right shin in front of A's belly, laying his left leg next to A's right leg...
3. ...and making a pincer movement with the legs.
4. He then turns A over onto his back using his arms. D is now in the mounted position.

1. D is holding A in the guard position. D opens his guard.
2. A hunches himself quite small so that D has difficulty in getting his shin in front of A's belly.
3. D places his left foot in front of A's right knee.
4. D pushes A's right knee back hard with his left foot and pulls A forcibly forwards and left...
5. ...and turns A over to the left onto his back. D is now in the mounted position.

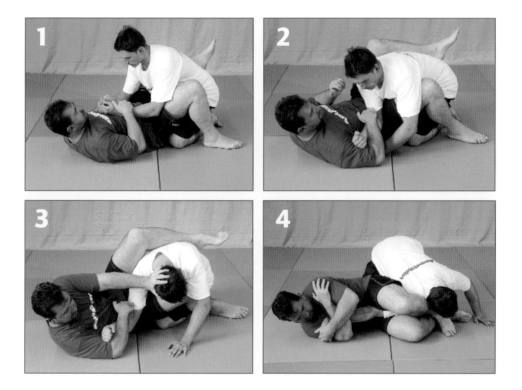

1. D is holding A in the guard position. D opens his guard.
2. D brings A's right arm diagonally over to his right side...
3. ...and pushes A's head away with his left hand...
4. ...swinging his left leg to the front of A's neck and executes a stretched arm lock.

Half Guard

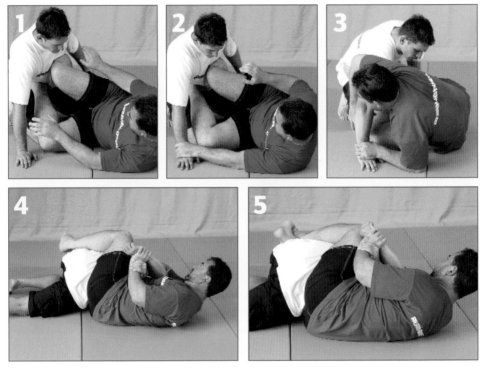

1. D is lying on the left side of his body in front of A, who is kneeling. D has placed his left leg into the groin and the right instep is placed on the right hand side of the upper body at about the height of the hips. D can keep A at a distance with his left leg.

2. A has placed his right arm down on the ground. D grabs hold of A's right lower arm just above the wrist with his left hand...

3. ...and lifts his upper body upwards to the left and grabs hold of his own left wrist round and over A's right upper arm with his right arm...

4. ...and brings his own hips outwards to the left and lies on his right hand side. As he does this he pushes A's right knee to the rear with his left leg so that A is forced onto his stomach.

5. D applies an arm lock (bent arm lock, Americano, Ude Garami, Kimura) by pushing the bent arm in the direction of the left shoulder.

Note: In the end phase, D should be lying on his right hand side so that he can apply the correct amount of pressure against the upper arm. If D is only lying on his back it will require lots more force to apply a successful technique.

Both Legs are between A's Legs

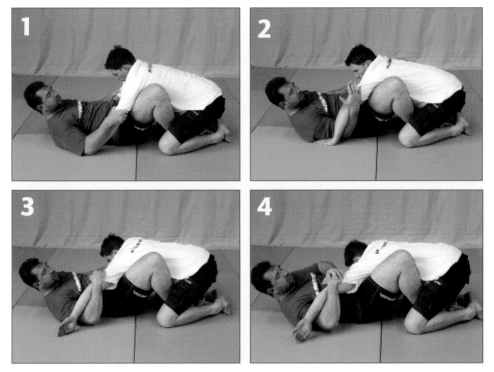

1. D is lying in front of A and has hooked both of his legs between A's legs. In this position D can grab hold of both of A's upper arms and keep his distance (by pushing away, pulling, lifting A up with the legs). A has lifted up his upper body (45°).

2. D also lifts up his body and pushes the right arm through under A's left arm...

3. ...grabs round A's left arm and places the right hand on A's left elbow...

4. ...places the left hand on his own right hand...

5. ...and pushes the right knee to the rear with the left leg so that A is forced onto his stomach.

6. D ends the combination by applying a stretched arm lock. D lies on his left side as he does this and has A's left arm lying close by the right hand side of his neck. The right knee is placed against A's left upper arm and is also pressing downwards.

One Leg is between the Legs and One Leg is in A's Groin

1. D is lying on his back with his right leg between A's legs and his left foot placed in A's groin. A is kneeling in front of D. Using his left foot D can keep his distance from A. At the same time it is important that D can control A's right arm by using both hands. D can pull A towards him, push him away or by using his right leg he can push him up. In the latter, D would also have to keep hold of A's left arm with his right arm.

2. A pushes his left arm through underneath D's right knee.

3. D makes use of this move by laying his right leg over A's head...

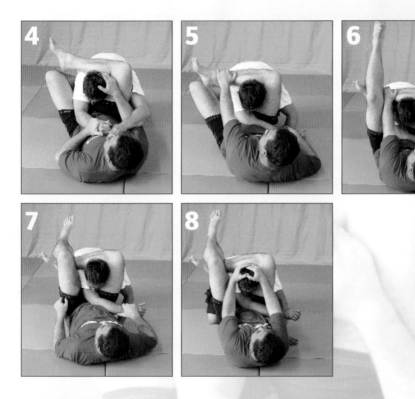

4. ...and pulls A's right arm in the direction of his right groin...
5. ...keeping hold of his own right lower leg with his left hand to prevent A from being able to stand up.
6. He stretches out his left leg...
7. ...and places it over the right instep at about the height of the hollow at the back of the knee.
8. D grabs hold of the right foot with his left hand and pulls it further into the hollow at the back of the left knee, pulls the right instep up and presses the heels in the direction of the ground. D moves his body over to the left and applies a stranglehold with his legs (Sangaku, Triangle, Figure Four). In addition, D can take hold of the back of A's head and pull it downwards while stretching out his hips. This results in effecting a stronger stranglehold technique and also effects the application of a neck lock. Instead of doing a neck lock, D can also take hold of the left leg from underneath with his right hand and increase the pressure this way.

Escape from the Guard Position

1. A has hold of D in the guard position and has clamped both of D's arms from the outside. The palms of D's hands are resting on the mat, face down behind A's shoulders.
2. D lifts himself up onto his feet, pushes this bottom up towards the ceiling and pushes forwards. While doing this D places his head forward on the ground...
3. ...and tries to get at least one arm free from the grip. D must leave his arms loose. If he tenses his arms and does it with force then he will have great difficulty in freeing his arms.
4. D holds himself up once free, first of all to one side.

5. A opens his guard in order to protect his genital area.

6. D brings his left arm through under A's right lower leg, places the right hand on A's shin and takes hold of his own right wrist with his left hand...

7. ...and lies down on his right side. D places the left foot on the inside of A's right thigh and ends the combinations with a foot lever.

1. A has hold of D in the guard position.
2. D brings his head onto A's chest and pushes the arms upwards close to the armpits...
3. ...and stands up.
4. A opens his guard to protect his genital area. D keeps hold of A's legs using both arms and clamps both of the legs against his thighs (D creates an X shape).

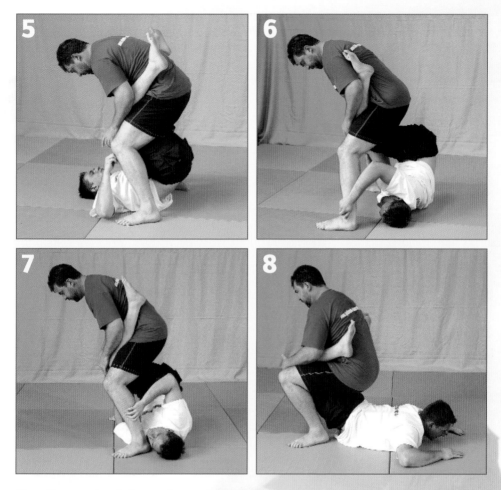

5. D now takes little running steps forwards over A...
6. ...causing A to have to turn round...
7. ...and land in the stomach down position.
8. D ends the combination with a mixture of a leg and spine lock.

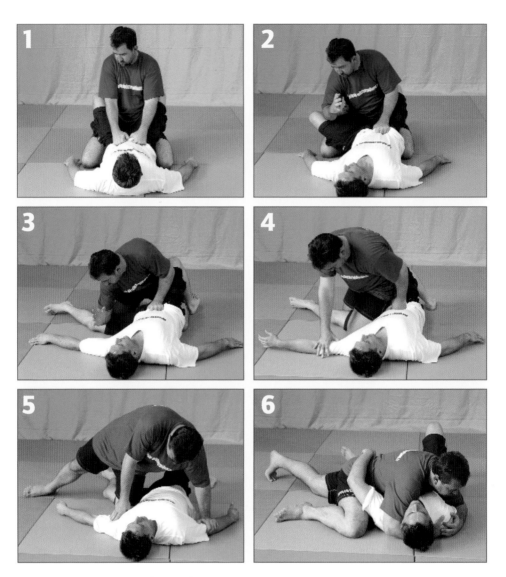

1. D is being held in A's guard.
2. D breaks out of the guard by boring the elbow into A's thigh near to the knee.
3. After D has opened the guard, D presses A's left thigh downwards...
4. ...pushes his left knee over A's left groin...
5. ...places his right leg out to the side...
6. ...and adopts the side mount/cross position.

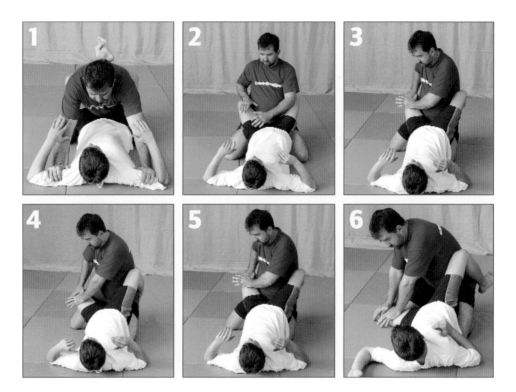

1. D lifts himself up and places his left knee underneath A's coccyx, leaning back hard so that the hips come forward. A could otherwise pull D's legs back downwards.

2. D places both hands in the region of the left knee...

3. ...and moves the leg with a rocking motion...

4. ...i.e., in a motion pulsing downwards. If D simply pushes downwards it is very difficult to free from the guard when confronting a strong opponent.

5.-6. D carries on doing the pulsating movements until A's left leg is on the ground.

Note: While applying pressure to the left knee, if D's hips give way, A can grab hold of him and pull back down again.

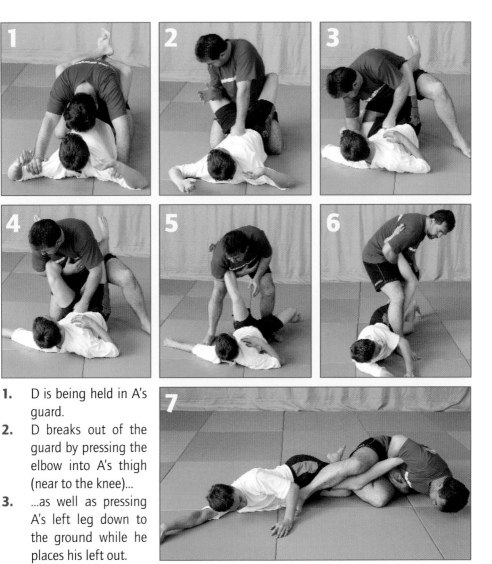

1. D is being held in A's guard.
2. D breaks out of the guard by pressing the elbow into A's thigh (near to the knee)...
3. ...as well as pressing A's left leg down to the ground while he places his left out.
4. D clamps his right arm round A's left thigh...
5. ...and stands right up...
6. ...putting his right foot over the stretched-up left thigh and places his foot down on the right hand side of A's upper body.
7. D lets himself fall down to the left side. He pins A's leg with his arms like in a leg lock. The body is lying at 45° to the ground.

1. A has hold of D in the guard position.
2. D brings his upper body close to A's upper body...
3. ...and places his fists on A's stomach...
4. ...and bumps himself in little movements to the rear until he can sit up.
5. D places both fists hard down into

the groin and the elbows close to the thighs.

Note: If D places his elbows outwards, A could counter with a bent arm lock (Americano, Kimura, Ude Garami). D places the right knee below A's coccyx and places the left leg at an angle of 45° to the left rear...

6. ...and presses the right thigh downwards with his elbow (just above the knee).

7. As he does this D rounds his body and places the left leg outwards 45° to the rear.

8. He now places the right foot underneath A's coccyx (while keeping both fists in A's groin) and slides the right lower leg/knee across A's right groin. The right hip is pushed well forward to the extreme as he does this. The right foot remains first of all hooked over the right thigh.

9. D places the left foot out at 90° to A...

10. ...and pulls the right leg up and across, adopting the cross position (Yoko Shio Gatame).

1. A has hold of D in the guard position.
2. D brings both of his arms between himself and...
3. ...A's legs...
4. lays his head on A's upper body...
5. ...and brings his own body backwards (thus breaking the guard).

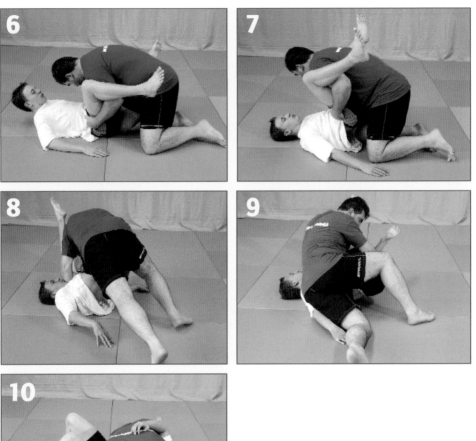

6.   D grabs round the legs and places the fingers round the outside into the groin...

7.   ...and pulls the seat of A's bottom upwards...

8.   ...turning A away to the right...

9.   ...placing his left hand next to the left hand side of A's head...

10. ...and adopts the cross position (Yoko Shio Gatame).

Note: This technique will also function if A has wrapped both of his legs round D's head.

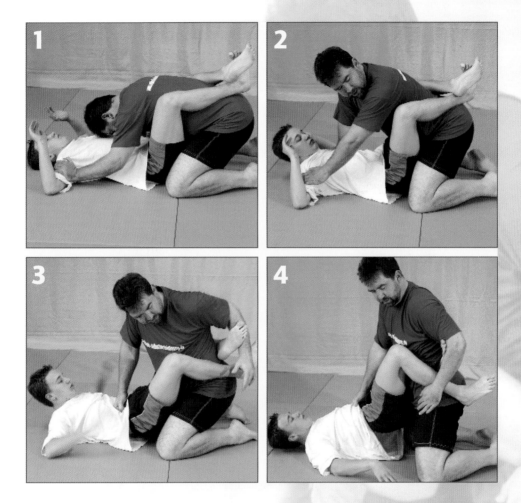

1. A is holding D in the guard position. D is pressing A's arms upwards while keeping his own arms close alongside A's body.
2. D glances quickly to the rear to establish which of A's crossed feet are on top.
3. If A's left foot is on top then D grabs hold of A's left foot with his left arm to the rear...
4. ...pulls it forward round his back and places a lever on it. The palm of his left hand lies close to his own body during this movement.

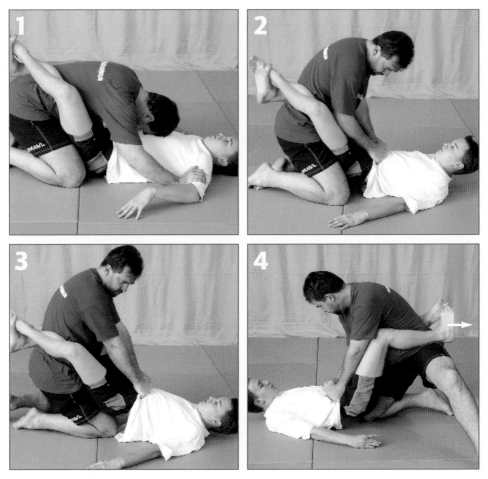

1. D is holding his head right down low with his face on A's stomach so that A cannot take an effective strike at D's face. One can cope with strikes to the back of the head more easily.
2. With both hands, D grabs hold of the pants at the waistband area...
3. ...presses the right knee into the buttocks...
4. ...puts his left leg out to the rear left 45° and with both elbows presses on both of A's thighs. D makes a rapid movement 45° away to the left rear.

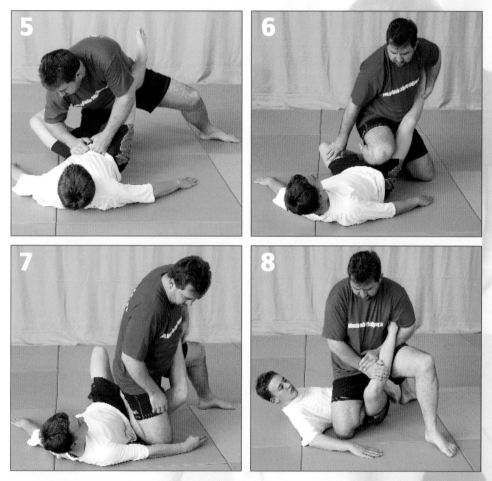

5.   ...and then places his right leg between A's legs and placing his foot close to or underneath A's buttocks.

6.   D slides his right lower leg over A's right groin so that D is now 90° to A.

7.   At the same time, D grabs hold of the right foot with the left hand and lays the palm of his left hand on his own chest. D's right instep is lying roughly in the area of the hollow of A's right knee. The left leg is placed stretched out forwards and propped up. Whether A twists round or not is immaterial regarding the effect. It is important, however, that the right knee is firmly on the ground.

8.   D places his right hand on A's right lower leg and he takes hold of the wrist with his left hand (locking position). To increase the pressure, D pushes his hips forwards.

Exercise

Playing round the Guarda (Ability to defend lying on the back)

1. D is lying on his back and A is front of him by his feet.
2. A now tries to get past the feet...
3. ...and D tries to prevent this by keeping his feet in front of A or placing his feet on A.

9.5　Mount Position

Completing Actions from the Mounted Position

The Arm Lock

1. D is sitting on A in the mounted position with his legs hooked round A's.
2. D places A's right arm underneath his left armpit (inside arm lock).
3. Then D slides his right knee over A's left biceps, supporting himself on the ground with his right hand.
4. D now places his right hand onto the right side of A's face and presses the head over onto the ground in the direction A's left shoulder.

5. D now climbs with his left leg over A's head and places his leg on the ground next to the head. The toes are pointing forward and the heel is just above A's neck. D keeps hold of A's right arm with an arm lock (inside).

1. D is sitting on A in the mounted position with his legs hooked round A's.

2. D places his left hand close to the left hand side of A's neck...

3. ...and pulls A's left arm, held on the outside, upwards with his right hand...

4. ...pushing the right hand through underneath A's left lower arm...

5. ...and places the left hand on A's left shoulder while taking hold of his own left wrist with his right hand and ends the combination with an **inside arm lock**.

1. D is sitting on A in the mounted position with his legs hooked round A's. D has pushed his head onto the ground against A's head.

2. D brings his arm over and round A's upper arm...

3. ...so that A's lower arms are under D's armpit and the fists are lying on A's stomach...

4. ...and pressing into A's stomach while he lifts up and ends the combination with **an inside arm lock**.

1. D is sitting on A in the mounted position with his legs hooked round A's. A's right arm is stretched out.

2. D grabs hold of A's right wrist with his left hand...

3. ...and places the right elbow close to the right hand side of A's head and along the right shoulder.

4. D now pushes his own right arm underneath A's right arm and takes hold of his own left wrist with the right hand and ends the combination with **an inside stretched arm lever**.

1. D is sitting on A in the mounted position with his legs hooked round A's.
2. D places his right hand (palm upwards) underneath A's outstretched left arm...
3. ...and brings A's left arm over A's head to the left with his right hand. A's left arm is now lying over his face.
4. D grabs hold of A's left wrist with his left hand...
5. ...and pushes down with his right arm through underneath A's left arm and grabs hold of his left wrist.

6. D pulls A's left arm towards his chest...
7. ...swings his right leg round in front of A's neck...
8. ...and places himself alongside A...
9. ...and ends the combination with a **sideways arm lock**.

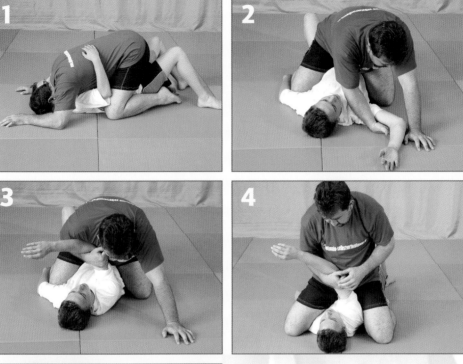

1. D is sitting on A in the mounted position with his legs hooked round A's.
2. D places his right hand underneath A's right upper arm...
3. ...and brings A's right arm diagonally over to the right.
4. Then D slides his right knee over A's left biceps.
5. D brings his right leg round A's head.

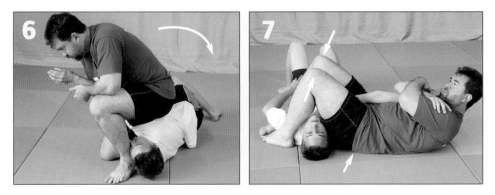

6. D places his left leg over A's head and puts his foot down onto the ground directly next to the head. The toes are pointing forwards and the heel is just above A's neck...

7. ...and he lets himself fall clockwise round to the left hand side into **a sideways arm lock**. D presses his knees together, lifts his hips up and pulls the arm downwards.

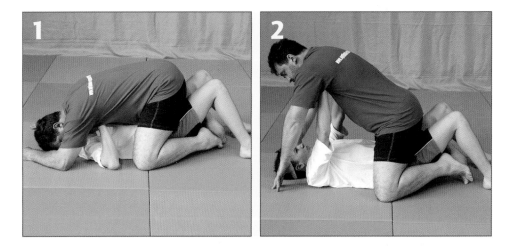

1. D is sitting on A in the mounted position with his legs hooked round A's.

2. A is pushing D up with both arms on D's chest.

3. D places both hands, one on the other, on A's chest...
4. ...pushes himself up and turns clockwise 90°...
5. ...and brings his right leg round over A's head...
6. ...and ends the combination with a sideways arm lock. When doing this, it is important that D presses his knees together, lifts his hips up and pulls the levered arm in the direction of the small finger over the groin towards the ground.

The Bent Arm Lock (Ude Garami)

1. D is sitting on A in the mounted position with his legs hooked round A's. D has placed his left arm next to the right hand side of A's upper body, just in front of A's upper arm that is angled downwards at 90° flat on the ground.

2. D lifts A's right elbow up with his left hand a little...

3. ...pushes his right arm through underneath A's right arm and at the same time lies over slightly to his right side. D grabs hold of A's right wrist with his left hand...

4. ...and takes hold of his own left wrist with the right hand...

5. ...pulls the bent elbow upwards and ends the combination with a bent arm lock **(Americano, Chicken Wing, Kimura, Ude Garami)**.

1. D is sitting on A in the mounted position with his legs hooked round A's. A's upper arm is angled upwards to the rear at 90° flat on the ground.

2. D grabs hold of A's right wrist with his right hand (or also the right hand if a bent hand lock is being applied) ...

3. ...pushes his left arm through underneath A's right upper arm and takes hold of his own right wrist...

4. ...pulls A's right arm in the direction of A's right hip...

5. ...and tips the elbow upwards ending the combination with a bent arm lock **(Francesa, Ude Garami)**.

The Neck Lock

1. D is sitting on A in the mounted position with his legs hooked round A's.
2. D places his right elbow right up by the right side of A's head...
3. ...and presses the head up to the right with the elbow...
4. ...further in the direction of A's chest, bringing his right hand under A's left upper arm and placing it underneath A's left shoulder blade.
5. D ends the combination with a neck lock.

6. Addition to the previous combination

D brings his right leg over A's upper body along the right hand side of the body and pushes his right knee underneath A's right upper arm.

1. D is sitting on A in the mounted position with his legs hooked round A's.

2. D brings his right arm underneath the back of A's neck, lays the right hand on his own left biceps...

3. ...and the left hand on A's forehead. D places his own face on the back of the left hand and pushes A's neck to the rear with his shoulder/chest (which is just underneath A's chin).

4. As he does this he presses his right arm upward and the left hand downwards. As far as possible D holds his legs well apart and hooked round A's.

1. D is sitting on A in the mounted position with his legs hooked round A's. D has placed both of his arms on the ground above A's arms.

2. D places his right elbow next to the right hand side of the top of A's head (to get a better leverage) and his hand is near to A's shoulder.

3. D pushes the head forwards and upwards with his elbow...

4. ...brings his right arm round behind A's neck...

5. ...and places the right hand on A's stomach below his own stomach. D lays his head (top of the skull) forwards onto the ground to provide a support.

6. D takes hold of his own right hand with his left hand and pushes himself forwards strengthening the neck lock as he does this.

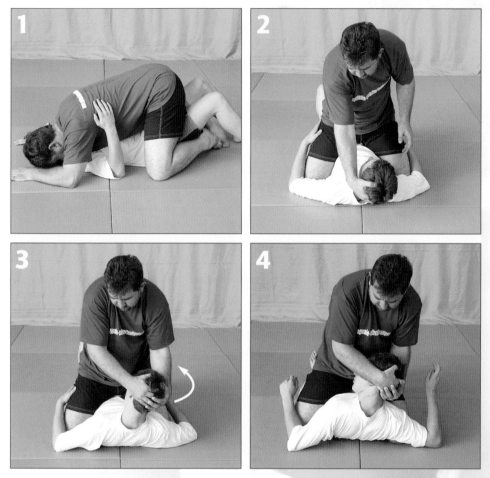

1. D is sitting on A in the mounted position with his legs hooked round A's.
2. D grabs hold of the top of the back of A's head with the right hand...
3. ...and pulls the head up...
4. ...taking hold of the head with the left hand as well. D then pulls A's head onto his chest (slightly in the direction of his left thigh) and ends the combination with a neck lock.

Stranglehold Techniques

1. D is sitting on A in the mounted position with his legs hooked round A's.
2. D pushes his right arm underneath the nape of A's neck...
3. ...lays his left lower arm on A's throat...
4. ...and takes hold of his own right lower arm with his left hand on the outside and ends the combination with a stranglehold using the arms.

1. D is sitting on A in the mounted position with his legs hooked round A's.
2. D brings A's right arm diagonally across A's throat...
3. ...pushes his right arm underneath A's neck...
4. ...and pins down A's right upper arm by pushing his head (right hand side of the face) against the upper arm...
5. ...pushes the right arm further inwards with the left hand and places the right hand on his left biceps...
6. ...and places his left hand on A's head, ending the combination with a stranglehold using the arms.

Escape from the Mounted Position

Freeing Both Legs

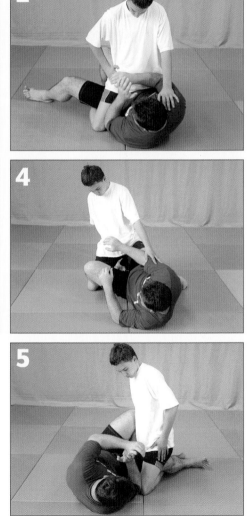

1. A is sitting on D in the mounted position.
2. D lies slightly over onto the left side of his body, presses his left elbow against A's right thigh and tries to bring his leg back.
3. If he manages to do this, he then places his right hand (in addition to his left hand) on A's right thigh and pushes the leg with both hands further to the rear.
4. As soon as he has gained enough room, D pulls his left leg through underneath A's right leg so that the instep of the left foot is on A's right thigh.
5. D now turns over onto his right side, pushes against A's left thigh with his elbow and tries to bring his leg back.

6. If he successfully does this, he then places his left hand (in addition to his right hand) on A's left thigh and pushes the leg with both hands further to the rear.

7./8. D now grabs round A's back with both arms and pulls A downwards.

9. D lifts his own legs up so that A is balancing horizontally in the air...

10. ...and turns him over to the right.

11. Now D is in the mounted position.

Freeing One Leg

1. A is sitting on D in the mounted position.
2. D lies slightly over onto the left side of his body...
3. ...presses his left elbow against A's right thigh and tries to bring his leg back.
4. If he manages to do this, he then places both hands on A's right thigh

and pushes the leg with both hands further to the rear. As soon as he has gained enough room, D pulls his left leg through underneath A's right leg so that the instep of the left foot is on A's right thigh.
5. D now turns over onto his right side...

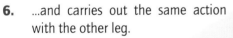

6. ...and carries out the same action with the other leg.

7. D pulls the left leg completely out and places it next to A's right leg...

8. ...stretches his left arm and pins A's right arm stretched out outwards and to the rear.

9. D now, first of all, turns over a little onto his left side and turns A to the left by pushing against A's left

thigh with his hooked-in right leg while at the same time executing a scissor movement with the left leg...

10. ...and now is in the mounted position on A as a result.

1. A is sitting on D in the mounted position and is lifting up the upper body.
2. D places his feet close to A's bottom and places both of his fists on A's stomach...
3. ...and pushes upwards...
4. ...pushing the left leg through underneath A's right leg...
5. ...so that D's lower leg is lying on the inside of A's thigh and the left foot is hooked around the back of the thigh.

6. D swivels round 90° clockwise to the right...

7. ...swings his right leg inwards over A's left leg so that A (seen from his viewpoint) is made to fall down to the right.

8. D has A's left foot under his armpit and has placed his own right foot close against A's stomach. D presses down onto A's left leg with his right knee and pins down the left lower leg with the right arm.

9. D pushes the right lower arm through underneath A's left calf and holds A in a leg lock.

10. D turns over counterclockwise onto his stomach.

Escape by Using the Bridge

1. A is sitting on D in the mounted position and has his right lower arm under the back of D's neck and he tries to apply a stranglehold with his arms.
2. D presses his head hard down onto the ground so that A cannot remove his arm and lean up on it to effect a counter movement. D brings his feet up close to the backside...
3. ...and pins the right arm down at the elbow with his left hand (so that A cannot get his arm out from underneath the neck). With his left foot, D pins A's right foot down (so that A cannot place his leg out sideways)...
4. ...and places his right hand on A's left hip and pushes the hips up...

5. ...turns over to the left pressing up A's hip for support with his right hand, taking care that A cannot pull his right arm out from underneath his head...
6. ...and is back into the guard position.

1. A is sitting on D in the mounted position and is applying a stranglehold with both hands.
2. D grasps hold of A's lower arms close to the wrists with both hands and places his own legs close to his own backside...
3. ...rips his hips up quickly...
4. ...turns over to the left and is now in A's guard position.
5. D pushes his body backwards thus releasing himself from the grip round his throat.

1. A is sitting upright on D in the mounted position.
2. D rips his hips up quickly (forming a bridge). A loses his balance from this movement and has to support himself with both hands on the ground just above D's head.
3. D wraps his left arm round A's right arm (counterclockwise direction)...
4. ...and places his left hand in the bend of A's elbow. D snatches A's right arm round onto his left side of the upper body, places the right hand behind A's elbow (so that he cannot pull his arm out), pins A's right foot down with his left foot...

5. ...lifts his hips up in a rapid movement and turns over on the left shoulder...
6. ...and is back in the mounted position.

9.6 On the Back/On All Fours/Back Mount

Completing Actions from the All Fours Position/Back Mount

1. A is on all fours.
2. D is on the right hand side of A. The right arm is grasping hold of A's upper arm furthest away and round the outside, while the left hand has hold of the left ankle.
3. D pulls the arms and legs towards him and at the same time pushes forward with his upper body...
4. ...so that A is down on his back and D immobilizes him there.

1. A is kneeling on the ground and supports himself in the bank position on both arms. D climbs onto A's back and hooks his legs round A's legs...

2. ...and pushes his hips forwards. The pressure exerted onto A's back forces him down onto his stomach.

3. D pushes his right arm underneath A's neck...

4. ...and places his right hand on his left biceps...

5. ...and then places his left hand on the left hand side of A's head with the right half of his own face on the back of his own hand. D moves his body forwards thus increasing the stranglehold.

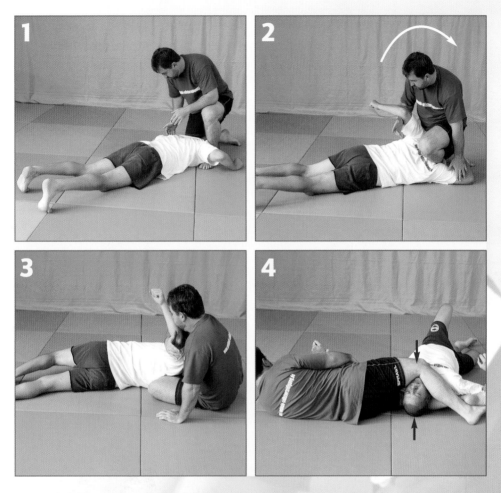

1. A is lying on his stomach in front of D.
2. D places his right knee next to the left hand side of A's head and places his left foot behind A's right upper arm.
3. D grasps hold of A's left arm and lets himself fall down to his left side.
4. D closes the legs and carries out a stranglehold with his legs (leg and neck scissors).

Escape by Attacking from the All Fours/Back Mount Position

1. D is on all fours in the bank position. A is kneeling in front of D and his left leg is propped up, the left arm is underneath D's right arm and laid on his back and his chin is laid on D's spine.

2. D now grasps hold of A's left upper arm just behind the elbow with his right arm and pins it down...

3. ...places his right leg out sideways, pushes his left leg to the outside past his own right leg...

4. ...and pushes his neck hard backwards.

5. D turns round clockwise further ...
6. ...until he is directly behind A. D now spreads both of his legs out in order to gain a good balance. From this point he can now execute further techniques.

1. D is on all fours. A is behind D and is grasping D round the body.
2. If A does not spread his legs i.e., he does not have a stable position, D can bring his right arm between his own legs...
3. ...and do a forward roll to the left.
4. D turns further until he is in the cross position (side mount/Yoko Shio Gatame).

9.7   Side Mount/Cross Position/Yoko Shio Gatame

Note: In Luta Livre, there is no difference made between the terms 'cross position' and 'side mount'. Both come under the main term 'side mount'. The side mount is also often called a 'scarf hold' – in this book we refer to the 'side mount'.

Description of the side mount (Kesa Gatame)

1. D lies on his side over A with his backside well tucked down. D's center of gravity is placed a little above A's hips and he holds his right arm close alongside A's left side in order to limit A being able to move about. The left hip is pushed close into the right hand side of A's body. D is keeping hold of A by applying pressure on both sides of his body. Since D is lying on his hip it is a relatively firm hold and allows plenty of room to carry out actions in a forward direction.

Description of the cross position (Yoko Shio Gatame/side mount)

1. D is lying with his stomach pressing down on A's upper body and with his backside well tucked in. D has placed his left knee underneath A's right shoulder and the right leg is stretched out to the rear. He keeps hold of A's left arm with his right arm.

Lead-up exercise

1. A is lying on D in the cross position (side mount) and is supporting himself firmly on the ground using both lower arms.
2. D tries to get A off or to get one of his legs between himself and A.
3. A can changeover his legs (e.g., like in the side mount).
4. As soon as all this is successful, then roles are changed over.
5. The exercise should be conducted in a playful manner.

Completing Actions from the Side Mount Position (Kesa Gatame), Cross Position (Yoko Shio Gatame)

The Arm Lock

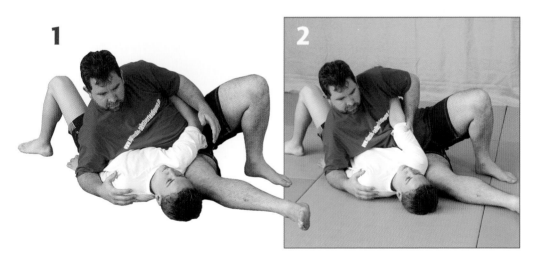

1. D is lying on his side over A in the side mount position (Kesa Gatame) and both of A's hands are free.
2. D grasps hold of A's upper arm in a circular motion counterclockwise with his left hand and brings A's hand under his left armpit, lays his left hand underneath A's elbow and keeps hold of the arm. The right arm is lying alongside the left hand side of A, whose body is now held firmly.

3. D places his left foot close to the left hand side of A's head...

4. ...pulls his left shoulder to the rear, pressing the left leg against A's outstretched arm, brings his left hip forwards and ends the combination with an arm lock.

1. D is lying on A in the cross position (side mount, Yoko Shio Gatame) and tries to apply a bent arm lock (the palm of A's hand is pointing towards the ceiling) on A's left arm.

2. A stretches out the left arm being attacked.

3. D exploits this movement and applies a lock on A's outstretched left arm by having his right arm directly under A's left elbow with the hand grasping the inside of his own elbow near to his own biceps. The left hand is grasping hold of the left lower arm close to A's left wrist. For this it is important that D is blocking A's left shoulder so that he cannot dodge away upwards and has no chance of moving upwards. It is important that A's elbow is pushed upwards, the shoulder is held down and that the wrist is being pressed down.

4. D can help himself in this by laying his head onto A's upper arm.

The Bent Arm Lock (Ude Garami)

1. D is lying on A in the side mount position. A's left arm is lying up to the left towards the head.

2. D grasps hold of A's left wrist with his left hand...

3. ...pushes the right arm through underneath A's left arm and takes hold of his own left wrist.

4. D pulls A's bent up arm in the direction of A's left hip. During this movement, the back of A's left hand is kept on the ground.

5. In the final position, D lifts his right lower arm, presses his wrist upwards thus increasing the bent arm lock (Ude Garami, Francesa).

1. D is lying on A in the side mount position. A's left arm is lying down to the left pointing towards the feet.

2. D grasps hold of A's left wrist with his right hand...

3. ...pushes the left arm through underneath A's left arm and pulls A's hand close to A's left hip...

4. ...brings the arm in the direction of A's left shoulder...

5. ...lifts the left arm up thus applying a bent arm lock (Ude Garami, Americano, Kimura). D presses A's left arm behind his back. D checks his legs so that the right leg is lying underneath A's right shoulder. As a result A comes up a little. D, however, keeps his head low and watches out that A doesn't come up too much.

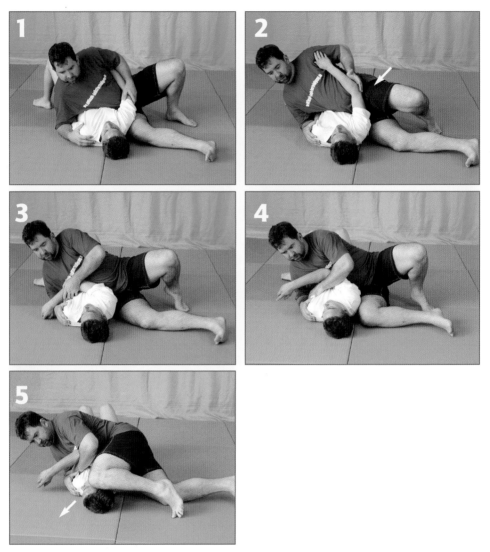

1. D is lying on A in the side mount position (Kesa Gatame - scarf hold). A has placed his right arm round D's left hip.
2. D pushes his hips firmly forward...
3. ...and brings A's right arm over A's stomach and under his own.
4. D pushes his left lower arm underneath A's right lower arm...
5. ...pushes A's head in the direction of A's left shoulder with his left knee (D can also execute a kick with his left knee at A's head). D pins A's left arm close to A's upper body with his right arm. For this, the palm of the left hand is lying on A's left shoulder

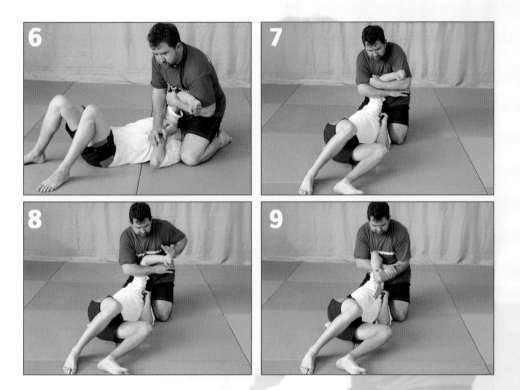

6. D places the left knee next to the left hand side of A's head and pulls the right knee close against A's back. A is now lying on his left side. D lifts his upper body upright and brings his left lower arm underneath A's right lower arm. D pulls A's arm up until it is at an angle of 90° to A's body.

7. D now changes over arms by bringing his right lower arm through underneath A's right lower arm...

8. ...and pins A's right lower arm against his upper body with his right lower arm...

9. ...grasps A's right wrist with his left hand and taking hold of his own left wrist with his right hand (bent arm lock, Ude Garami, Chicken Wing, Americano, Kimura)...

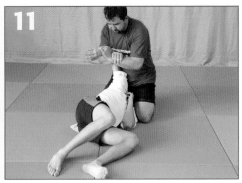

10. ...pulls the right upper arm very close to his upper body...
11. ...and brings the right arm outwards to the right...
12. ...and leads A's locked arm round behind his back or places A's right hand onto the right hand side of A's upper body and ends the combination with a bent arm lock. The bent arm lock can also be carried out on the ground behind A's back.

Note: If A holds onto his right hand with his left hand, then D can release the grip as described in the following sections.

Continuing the Action 1:

1. D counters by trying to pull the arm to the right.
2. A blocks this action by pulling his arm back. D exploits the energy produced by this by pushing A's right arm downwards to the left...
3. ...pulls the right arm up rapidly in a circular motion (counterclockwise) upwards...
4. ...and further round to the outside right...
5. ...and brings the locked arm up behind A's back.

Continuing the Action 2:

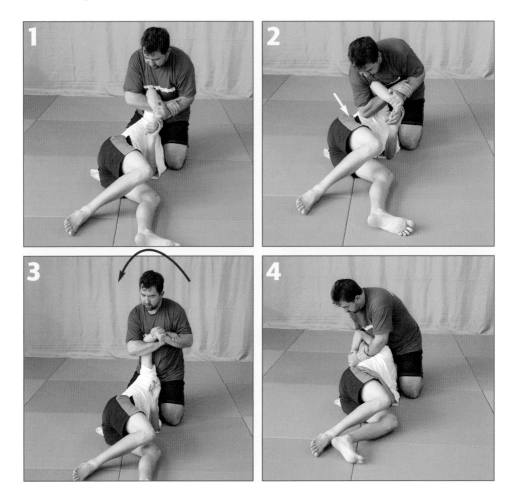

1. A holds onto his own right hand with his left hand.
2. D places the tip of his right elbow against the right side of A's upper body (against the ribs) and pushes his elbow hard into the ribs.
3. A loosens his grip and D can bring the locked arm upwards..
4. ...and then bring it round the outside behind A's back.

Continuing the Action 3:

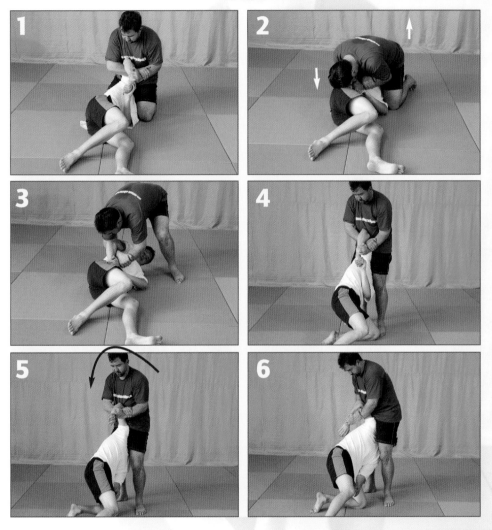

1. A holds onto his own right hand with his left hand.
2. D brings the whole weight of his body to bear on A's angled right upper arm and takes the weight off his feet...
3. ...jumps up from kneeling onto his feet...
4. ...pulls A up between his legs in a rapid movement...
5. ...brings A's locked right arm upwards...
6. ...and then out to the right. D ends the combination with a bent arm lock (Ude Garami, Chicken Wing, Americano).

The Neck Lock

1. D is lying on A in the side mount position (Kesa Gatame – scarf hold) and both of A's hands are free...

2. D reaches underneath A's head (at the top of the head) with his left lower arm...

3. ...propping himself up with his right elbow on A's ribcage...

4. ...takes hold of his own left hand with his right hand and pulls the head forward. In doing this, D exerts a lot of pressure against A's ribcage. The neck lock is achieved by pulling forward.

Stranglehold Techniques

1. D is lying on A in the cross position (side mount, Yoko Shio Gatame). Both of A's arms are under D's upper body.
2. D's left arm is underneath A's neck and he lifts A's upper body up...
3. ...brings it forward...
4. ...and then D gets round behind his back...

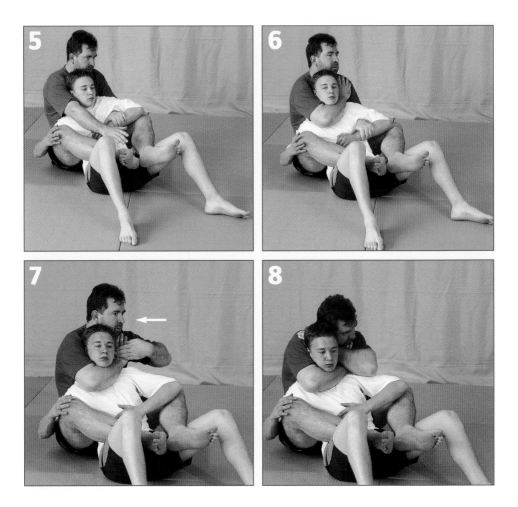

5. ...and places both legs over A's thighs...

6. ...and applies a stranglehold grip with the lower arm (Mata Leao). For this, D puts his right arm well round A's throat and neck, placing his right hand on his left shoulder...

7. ...pushes the left hand behind A's head (back of the hand is against the back of the head)...

8. ...and tenses the muscles of the upper arm and the upper back together.

1. D is on top of A in the side mount position (Kesa Gatame – scarf hold).
2. A presses against D's upper body with his left hand and tries to push him backwards.
3. D pushes A's left arm inwards with his right hand...
4. ...bends forward over A...
5. ...and pushes his left arm through underneath A's neck (70% of the technique). D inches his fingers further over the mat until he can't go any further...
6. ...and takes hold of his own left hand with his right hand, changes over legs so that they are spread out (D is now not lying sideways on A anymore, but more on his own stomach) and applies pressure towards A's left shoulder with his upper body, ending the combination with a stranglehold technique with A's own lower arm.

Escape from the Side Mount Position (Kesa Gatame), Cross Position (Yoko Shio Gatame)

1. A is lying on D in the cross position (side mount, Yoko Shio Gatame).
2. D brings his hips up rapidly so that he can get his right arm underneath A's upper body as the lift occurs.
3. D manages to get his right arm between himself and A and places his right hand on A's back.
4. D places both of his legs up and out and 'catapults' his hips up...

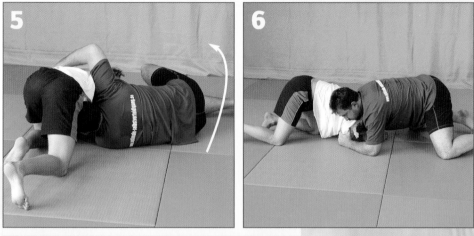

5. and turns counterclockwise through underneath A from this position.

6. The right arm immediately grabs round the neck...

7. ...and he ends the combination with a stranglehold technique using the arms (Guillotine).

1. A is on top of D in the cross position (side mount, Yoko Shio Gatame) and is trying to lever D with a bent arm lock (Ude Garami, Americano, Kimura).

2. D turns his hips so that the side of the left leg is lying flat on the ground.

3. D now grabs hold of the pants – as far to the inside as possible – with his left hand and then bends the left leg up again. This means that the bent arm lock is virtually ineffective.

4. D 'bumps' A up quickly...

5. ...in order then to turn onto his left side and push his right arm from the inside between A's head and A's right arm so that he can then get hold of the head round the right hand side of it.

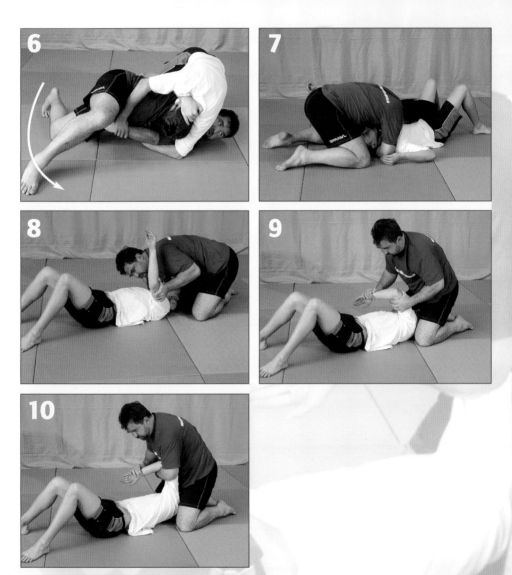

6. D pushes himself up with his legs, turns round counterclockwise quickly and scrabbles round A in this direction while A is turned over (rolled over).

7. D now kneels over A from the head end and lets go of his own pants in his left hand...

8. ...and grabs round A's left arm from the outside.

9. D grabs hold of A's left wrist with the right hand...

10. ...and pulls the arm close towards his upper body...

11. ...brings the left knee close to the left hand side of A's upper body...

12. ...swings the right leg over A's neck and ends the combination with a stretched arm lock (Juji Gatame). For this, D presses both of his knees together, lifts his hips up and pulls the arm over his stomach or over his left groin.

Note: The escape technique (from Point 5) will only work if A is not holding D's right hand shoulder!

1. A is lying on D in the cross position (side mount, Yoko Shio Gatame).
2. D pushes his hips up rapidly...
3. ...in order to be able to get his right lower arm down into A's groin.
4. D now manages to get it in by applying pressure with the lower arm and pushes his hips out backwards to the right (45°)...
5. ...pulls his right knee through underneath A...
6. ...and pushes himself backwards and is then in the guard position.

1. A is lying D in the side mount position (Kesa Gatame). A's legs are placed such that D cannot grasp round them with his legs, but without having both of them in front of D's head.

2. D 'cuddles' closely up to A and brings his right elbow onto the ground, grabbing round the hips with the left arm and taking hold of his own right wrist...

3. ...and pulls A in a semi-circular movement, first of all, in the direction of his left shoulder (diagonally 45° to the rear and left)...

4. ...and then further round towards his left hip...

5. ...until A is lying by D's side.

6. Finally, D adopts the cross position side mount, Yoko Shio Gatame).

1. A is lying on top of D in the side mount position (Kesa Gatame). A's legs are both lying on the ground around the height of A's head.
2. D brings his right arm onto the left hand side of A's body, pushes himself away and brings his legs counterclockwise to the left...
3. ...until he is in a position 180° to A...
4. ...and places his left hand on A's head...
5. ...pushes himself up and...
6. ...brings A down onto his back so that D is in the side mount position (Kesa Gatame).

1. A is lying on top of D in the side mount position (Kesa Gatame). A's legs are both lying close to those of D.
2. D 'cuddles' closely up to A and brings his left leg over A's left leg...
3. ...pushes his right leg through under A's left leg...
4. ...and grips round A's left leg with both legs. D puts his right elbow down on the ground, grasps round A's hip with his left arm and takes hold of his own right wrist with his left hand.
5. D turns A to the left...
6. ...and is then, himself, in a side mount (Kesa Gatame).

1. A is lying on top of D in the cross position (side mount). D has placed his left lower arm on the left hand side of A's neck.
2. D presses the left arm against A's neck...
3. ...pushes his backside up to the left...
4. ...brings his left thigh in front of the left hand side of A's neck...
5. ...and then brings the left instep underneath and into the hollow behind the back of his own right knee...
6. ...pulls the right lower leg downwards and grasps A's right wrist with his left hand and pins A in a stranglehold technique using his legs (Sangaku, Figure Four, Triangle). For this, A's right arm must lie in front of A's left groin.

9.8   The North-South Position

Completing Actions from the North-South Position

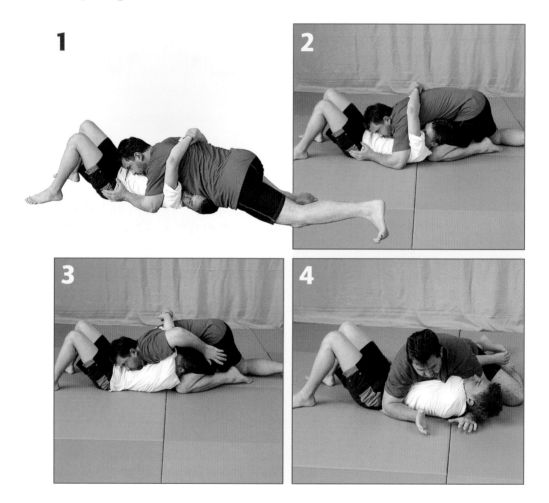

1.   A is lying on his back and D is on top from the other end. A's legs and feet are pulled up and he has both arms grasping round D's upper body below the arms.
2.   D brings his left knee to the right over A's head and places it close to the head.
3.   Then, using a lot of swing, D brings his left arm...
4.   ...backwards and then forwards again round A's head.

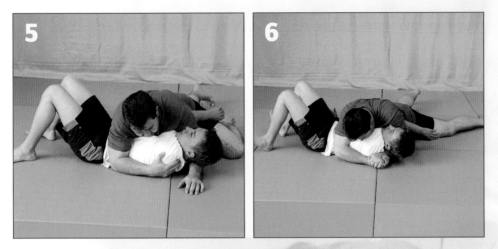

5. D lays his right arm close to A's left hand side...

6. ...and now takes hold of his own left hand with his right hand, pushes himself to the rear and tightens the grip. For this, A's left arm is underneath D's left armpit.

1. A is lying on his back and D is on top from the other end. A's left arm is lying on his stomach.

2. D grasps hold of A's left wrist with his right hand...

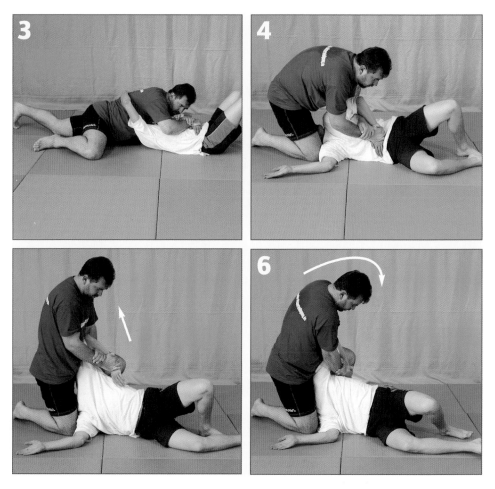

3. ...pushes his left arm through underneath A's left arm and takes hold of his right wrist. A keeps hold of his left hand with his right hand.

4. D props his left leg up, pulls A onto his side by pulling him up with the left arm. The right knee is close next to A's head.

5. D presses his left elbow into A's ribs. This causes pain so that A loosens his grip. Another way to get him to loosen the grip would be to pull the levered arm up rapidly and hard.

6. D brings the levered arm behind A's back and ends the combination with a bent arm lock (Americano, Kimura, Chicken Wing, Ude Garami).

Escape from the North-South Position

1. A is lying on D in the 'north-south' position.
2. D places both hands into A's groins...
3. ...presses into the groins with the fingers and pushes A away...
4. ...and then executes a backward roll onto A...
5. ...and pushes both legs underneath A's legs...

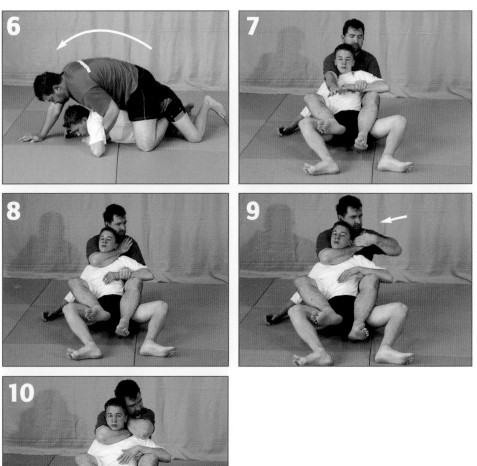

6.   ...grasps through between the left hand side of the body and the left arm (under the armpit) and grasps hold of the left lower arm.

7.   D turns A with him to the right so that D is now on his back and A is between his legs.

8.   D brings his right arm round in front of A's neck and lays the hand on his left shoulder.

9.   D pushes his left hand behind A's head (with the back of the hand facing the head)...

10.   ...and applies a stranglehold (Mata Leao).

Variation (from Point 8):

8. If A manages to protect the right hand side of his face with the right arm so that D cannot grasp behind A's head, then D reacts as follows:

9. D pushes the head from the left hand side to the right with the right hand...

10. ...swings his right leg round from the left hand side of the leg in front of A's head...

11. and applies a stretched sideways lock (arm lock, Juji Gatame).

1. A is lying on D in the 'north-south' position.
2. D places both hands into A's groins...
3. ...presses into the groins with the fingers and pushes A away...
4. ...lifts his legs up so that they are at right angles up in the air...
5. ...and swings them down to his left onto the ground...

6. ...pushes them back up again rapidly into the air...

7. ...and drops them down onto his right side...

8. ...and at the same time pushing A's right hip away with his hands...

9. ...turns to the left through underneath A (and also pulls his right leg through under A) and is then in the guard position.

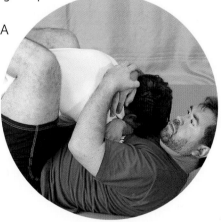

9.9 Transition from the Holding Technique to the Holding Technique Using the Stranglehold or Locking Technique

1. A and D each are holding the other's opposing wrist with the left hand.
2. D brings A's right arm over to his right hand and lets go with the left hand...
3. ...and gets behind A's back...
4. ...and grasps round A's upper body...
5. ...bringing his right leg round A's right leg...
6. ...hooks back with the right leg so that A topples forward onto his stomach...
7. D also hooks in the left leg under A's left leg, brings A onto his stomach and brings his right arm round A's neck...

8. ...places the right hand on his left shoulder and pushes the left hand with the back of the hand up against the back of A's head....

9. ...and applies a stranglehold technique using the lower arms.

10. Then D gets round to A's right side...

11. ...loosens the grip taking hold of A's upper arm with the right hand...

12. ...pulls it inwards so that A is now on his back.

13. D is in the cross position (side mount, Yoko Shio Gatame), and grabs hold of A's right wrist with his right hand and angles the right arm up...

14. ...and pins A with a bent arm lock (Ude Garami).
15. D brings his left knee onto A's stomach...
16. ...slides with the leg over the stomach and gets into the mount position.
17. Now, D brings his right arm under A's neck...
18. ...places the right hand on his own left biceps...
19. ...and places the palm of the hand on A's face with his own head on the back of the left hand. D then places the right shoulder under A's chin and executes a neck lock.

20. A pins D's right upper arm with his left hand and also pins D's right leg by placing his left leg in front of it...

21. ...and then lifts his hips up rapidly and turns D over onto his back.

22. D uses this counter by A and therefore has A now in a kidney lock with his legs (guard position).

23. D places his right leg out...

24. ...and places the left leg next to A's right leg.

25. D pushes the right leg in front of A's left groin...

26. ...and turns A over onto his back...
27. ...so that D is in the mount position again.
28. D places his right arm under A's neck...
29. ...brings his right leg also onto A's right hand side, watching out that A's right hand is kept close to his body...
30. ...and is now in the cross position (side mount, Yoko Shio Gatame).
31. A tries to lift up his upper body. D uses A's counter and lays his left arm round A's neck, lifts the upper body up...

32. ...and gets round behind his back.
33. D places the legs on the inside of A's thigh (not crossed over otherwise A could use a foot lever)...
34. ...and brings the right arm in front of A's throat...
35. ...lays the right hand on his left shoulder...
36. ...pushing the left hand behind A's head (back of the hand towards the head)...
37. ...and ends the combination with a stranglehold (Mata Leao).

9.10   Stranglehold Techniques (Chokes)

Completing Actions from Strangleholds with the Arms

1. A lies between D's legs in the guard position.
2. A lays his right lower arm against D's throat, lifts up onto his feet and applies a strong pressure on D's throat.
3. D stretches his hips for a short while...
4. ...and, at the same time, slaps A's right arm against his right hand side with his left hand.

5. D pulls his legs back again and lays the right arm round A's neck...

6. ...takes hold of his own right hand with his left hand by hooking his fingers together and now opens his legs from the guard position...

7. ...grips A's legs between his legs and turns to the left...

8. ...and lies down on the ground close next to A. In this, D brings his nose down onto the ground and presses his right ear firmly against A's right upper arm and now tightens the grip.

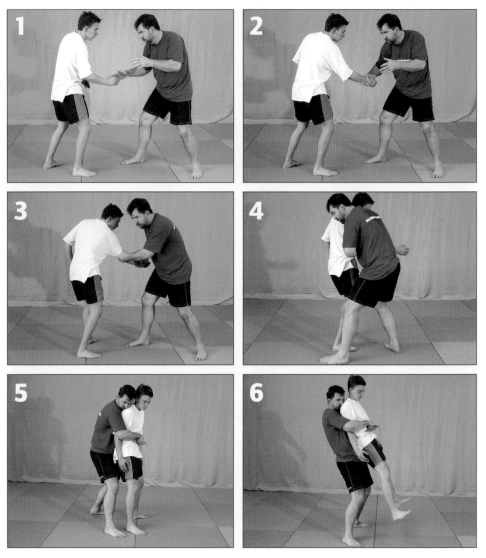

1. A is standing opposite D.
2. D grabs hold of A's right wrist with his right hand.
3. D grabs hold of the right upper arm just above the right elbow with his left hand and pulls A forwards...
4. ...and, at the same time gets round behind A.
5. D grasps round A's upper body around the belt line...
6. ...and lifts A up about 20 cms from the ground...

7. ...puts him down again and A sags at the knees.

8. D lets himself fall backwards. D pins down A's thighs with both of his legs.

9. D lays his right arm round A's throat and lays his hand on his own left shoulder...

10. ...pushing his right hand behind the back of A's neck. Not against the head, otherwise A could pull the hand down. D lays the back of the left hand onto his own right shoulder.

11. D brings his head forward close next to the left hand side of the back of A's head. The stranglehold (Mata Leao) is now gradually tightened (like a pair of pliers).

Note: The sequence in this technique is very important. If the stranglehold is done while standing, A could get free. First of all A must be pinned down before the stranglehold is applied.

1. A and D are standing opposite each other.
2. A tries to execute a double-handed leg sweep on D.
3. D dodges back and takes A's head onto his left upper body and places his left arm under A's right arm while the left hand is on A's back. The right hand is on A's back at this point.

4. D brings his left hand or his left lower arm upwards round A's throat.
5. D takes hold of his own left wrist with his right hand (not only the fingers!). D's head lies on A's back. D's left shoulder is laid very close onto A's back (tucked up). **Note:** The technique also works when standing. D now pulls his arms upwards to the right (the right elbow is pointing at the ceiling).

8. ...lays it in the hollow at the back of A's knee while D falls down sideways.

9. D turns right 180° until he is lying on A and has applied a stranglehold.

6. D kneels on the ground with his left knee and his right leg is propped out sideways. A is kneeling on his left leg and also has his right leg propped out sideways.

7. D swings his right leg round from the outside round A's left leg...

8. ...lays it in the hollow at the back of A's knee while D falls down sideways.

9. D turns right 180° until he is lying on A and has applied a stranglehold.

Note: Even when the turn isn't fully completed, this poses no problem, the stranglehold works anyway.

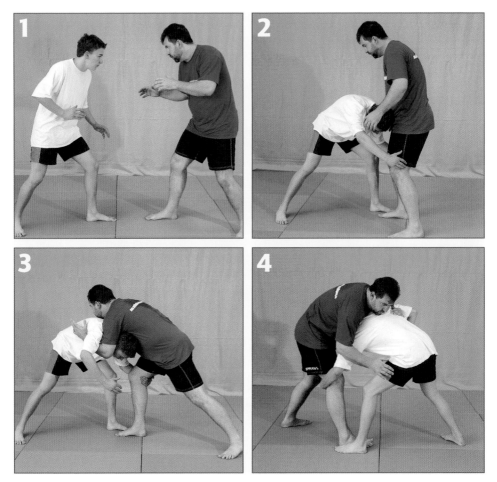

1. A and D are standing opposite each other.
2. A tries to execute a double-handed leg sweep on D and is standing with his left leg forward and has grasped hold of D's right leg in the area of the hollow at the back of the knee with his left hand.
3. D dodges back with his left leg and is keeping A's head on the left side of his upper body.
4. D grasps hold underneath A's right arm and lays the hand on A's back/side. The right hand is used, first of all, to effect a stop by blocking, putting it behind A's arm against A's left thigh and then it grasps over/behind A's left arm.

5.   D now pulls his right leg to the rear and thus breaks A's grip, A's arm is then, however, stretched out forwards. D presses diagonally inwards against A's outstretched left arm with his own right upper arm/elbow...

6.   ...and now grasps round A's neck with the left hand by bringing up his left lower arm round the neck and laying it on his own right biceps...

7.   ...and choking the throat hard. The right hand during this is lying on A's back.

8.   D now stretches himself out and goes down into the prone position. D inches along to the rear on his stomach, bit by bit and thus increases the stranglehold.

Note: It is important that A's left arm is lying stretched across in front of A's face/throat, because A's shoulder is being pushed up against his own throat. Any other way could mean that the stranglehold will not work properly.

Variation A for the previous exercise:

Everything up to and including Point 7

8.	D brings the outstretched right leg round A's legs...
9.	... and lets himself fall down to the right. The stranglehold is kept firm. On the ground then the hips are pushed forwards.

Variation B for the previous exercise:

Everything up to and including Point 7

8.	D brings the outstretched right leg round A's hips and lets himself fall down backwards i.e., D does a backward roll. D's leg is lying in the region of A's lumbar vertebra; the stranglehold is kept firm. On the ground the hips are then pushed forwards.

Note: It doesn't matter which direction one falls down in. This is of no consequence for the effectiveness of the technique. It is important, however, that the stranglehold is placed well and that D's leg is laid round A's legs/hips.

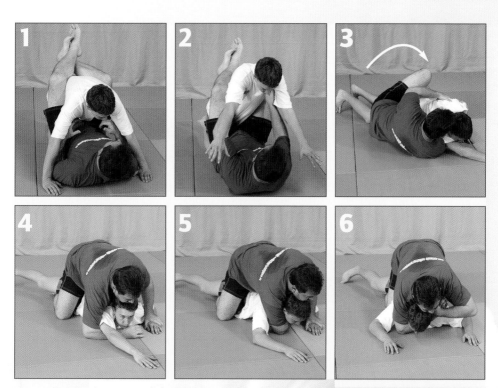

1. A is lying between D's legs in the guard position. Both of A's arms are placed out next to either side of D.
2. D presses A up with both hands placed on the side or next to A's armpits and lifts him up briefly...
3. ...so that D can slide through underneath A's right arm...
4. ...and grasps firmly round A's back. At the same time D lays his head close to A's upper body i.e., behind A's right shoulder. D now pushes his backside out to the left (without opening his legs!)

and, bit by bit, climbs up onto A until his legs are between A's legs. It is better, first of all, to get properly on top of A before one goes for the neck.
5. D now presses his hips forward so that A's legs are stretched out and up behind him and A's head is lifted up (higher than normal). D now pushes his right arm in front of A's throat and brings him onto his left shoulder (more in the direction of the upper chest muscles)...
6. ...lays the left arm over and behind the nape of A's neck...
7. ...and tenses his back muscles together choking A with the lower arms (Mata Leao).

217

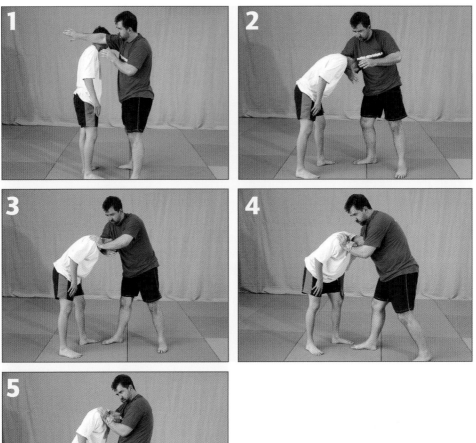

1. A is standing opposite D. D brings his right arm past the right hand side of A's head and wraps the arm round A's neck...
2. ...and pulls A's head downwards and brings the right arm round A's neck...
3. ...and places the left hand on A's right shoulder...
4. ...taking hold of his own left wrist with his own right hand.
5. If D now pushes his hips forward, the lever hold/stranglehold becomes effective.

1. A is standing opposite D. D grasps hold of the back of A's head with his right hand...
2. ...and the left hand grasps the chin...
3. and brings it underneath his left armpit (i.e., the back of D's right hand is now lying directly under his own armpit).
4. The left lower arm is brought from below up round A's neck. D's left hand grasps the right lower arm close to the wrist round the outside.
5. D keeps his legs together so that A will have difficulty to strike at the genital area. He then pushes his hips forward.

Escape from Strangleholds Using the Arms

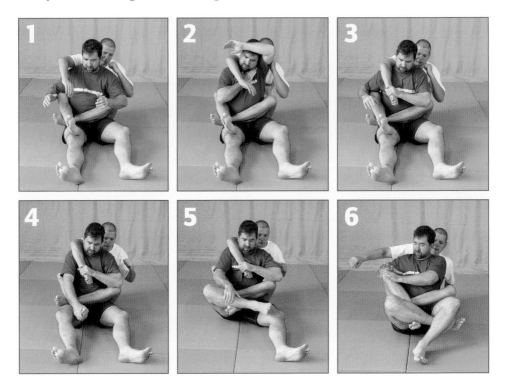

1. A is sitting behind D on the ground with his left leg round in front of D's stomach. A has placed his right leg at the rough area of the hollow at the back of the knee round over his own left instep (Figure Four, Triangle, Sangaku).

2. A tries to put his right arm round D's neck. D prevents this by placing his left upper arm up onto the left hand side of his head. D pushes the right hand between his left shoulder and the left side of his chin.

3. D grasps hold of A's right wrist with his left hand...

4. ...and grasps hold of the right foot with his right hand...

5. ...brings the right leg over his right thigh...

6. ...and places the right lower leg on A's right foot laying the left leg at the area of the hollow at the back of it on his own right instep. D then presses A's right foot downwards with the legs, supporting the whole action by pushing A's right knee down with both hands.

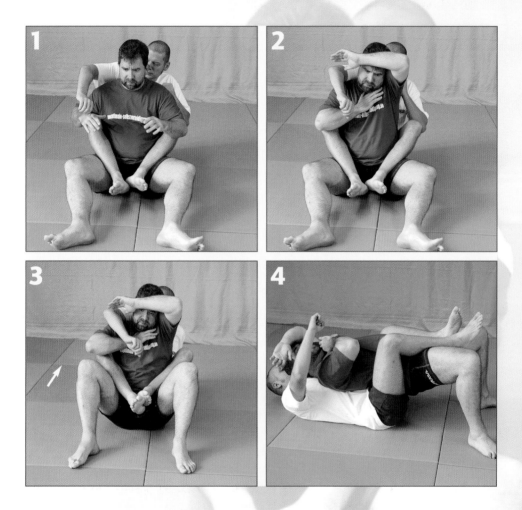

1. A is sitting behind D on the ground with both of his legs round over D's thighs.
2. A tries to put his right arm round D's neck. D prevents this by placing his left upper arm up onto the left hand side of his head and the lower part onto his forehead. D pushes the right hand between his left shoulder and the left side of his chin.
3. D pulls up both of his feet close towards his backside.
4. D pushes himself backwards so that A is now lying on his back.

5. D pushes his backside up to the left thus opening A's legs that were pinning him.
6. D pushes A's right knee outwards with both hands and pulls the right leg outwards...
7. ...and adopts the mount position.

1. A is sitting behind D on the ground with both of his legs round over D's thighs.
2. A tries to put his right arm round D's neck. D prevents this by placing his left upper arm up onto the left hand side of his head and the lower part onto his forehead. D pushes the right hand between his left shoulder and the left side of his chin.
3. D grasps hold of A's right foot with his right hand and brings it over A's left foot.
4. D places his right thigh onto A's right instep...
5. ...and lays his left leg at the area of the hollow at the back of it onto his right instep (Figure Four, Sangaku, Triangle)...
6. ...stretches himself and presses both hands against A's left knee. D pushes down with both legs so that A's ankle is levered. By pressing with both hands onto A's left knee the leverage is increased.

Note: If the opponent is inexperienced and has his feet crossed over from the beginning, D can start directly with Point 6.

Completing Actions from Strangleholds with the Legs

1. A is in D's guard.
2. A tries to release himself from the leg hold with his left arm, but is holding his right arm pressed against D's upper body.
3. D grasps hold of A's right arm with both hands...
4. ...pulls A's right arm onto the right hand side of his upper body and pins the arm with both hands against his upper body. Instead of Point 2, D can also pin down A's right arm with the left arm and grasp hold of the left hand side of A's head and push it to the left.

5. D now lays his right leg onto the nape of A's head...

6. ...brings A's right arm further to the left onto the right hip. This is necessary because later on this arm will strangle A. If the arm is not lying diagonally in front of A, it can occur that the technique does achieve the strangling effect. If need be D pulls the right foot still with the left hand further to the left and prevents A from standing up and escape himself.

7. D lays the left leg (at the hollow at the back of the knee) over the right ankle (Sangaku, Figure Four, Triangle). At this juncture, D can also still pull his right foot back with the left arm i.e., to get it properly into the hollow of the knee.

8. Finally, the knees are pressed together, the hips are lifted up and A's head is grasped in both hands and pulled downwards.

Note: If the Sangaku (Figure Four, Triangle) is not properly applied – then...

1. ...D grasps A's right arm with his right hand...
2. ...briefly loosen the grip...
3. ...but then still keeps hold of A's head with the left hand and pulls it over further in the direction 90° to A...
4. ...and continues with the leg clamp again.

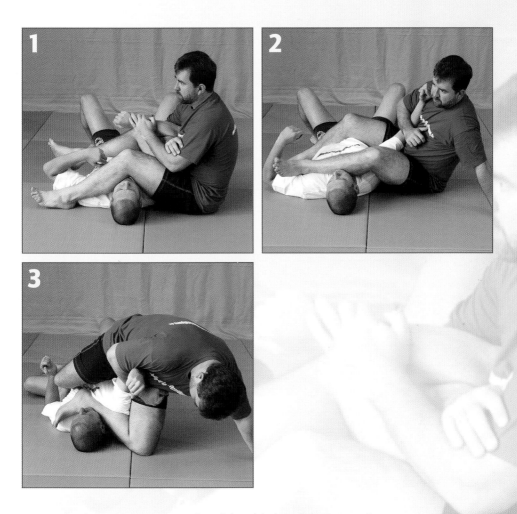

1. D is sitting on the ground and has his legs lying over A's upper body (like the entry to the stretched side-lock) and A is lying at right angles in front of D. A is holding his arm with his left hand, because D is trying to apply a stretch side-lock. D's right arm is lying in the crease of A's right elbow and the palm of the hand is on the left side of D's chest.

2. D leans backwards and props himself up on his left arm to the rear. He then turns his body a little to the left so that he is sitting on the left cheek of his backside.

3. D brings his left leg in front of A's throat so that D's left foot is lying on the left side of A's neck. D's right foot is lying close to the left hand side of A's upper body. D now brings the hips forward and chokes A with his left lower leg.

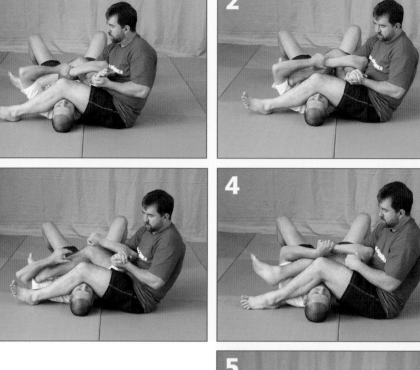

1. D is sitting on the ground and has his legs lying over A's upper body (like the entry to the stretched side-lock) and A is lying at right angles in front of D. A is holding his arm with his left hand, because D is trying to apply a stretch side-lock. D's right arm is lying in the crease of A's right elbow and the palm of the hand is on the left side of D's chest.

2. D places his right foot on A's upper arm...

3. ...and shoves A's left arm away kicking with his right leg.

4. ...A grasps hold of his right wrist with his left hand round D's right leg.

5. A now picks up momentum by lifting his legs slightly and then pushing himself up to the right until A gets onto his knees.

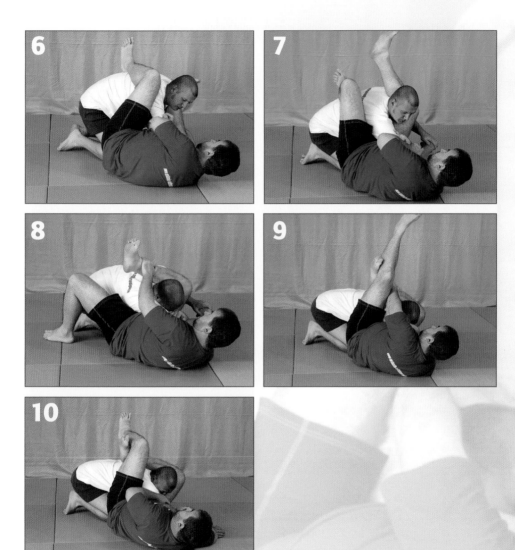

6. D now lifts his left leg over A's head...

7. ...pulls A's right arm diagonally in front of A onto D's hip...

8. ...lays his right leg diagonally behind A's neck and grasps his own right foot with his own right hand so that A cannot stand up...

9. ...lays the hollow behind the knee of his left leg over the right ankle (Sangaku, Figure Four, Triangle)...

10. ...and pulls his right foot into the hollow at the back of the left knee in order to increase the effect.

Starting Point: Continuing from the previous exercise:

There are fighters who try to break out free from the Triangle by standing up and then trying to drop their opponent from a height onto their neck or back, in the hope that the opponent releases the Triangle lock.

1. Just as A stands up...
2. ...D goes up into a handstand keeping the Triangle lock applied (Sangaku, Figure Four).

9.11 Stretching Locks (Stretched Arm Lock/Juji Gatame)

Completing Actions from the Stretched Arm Lock

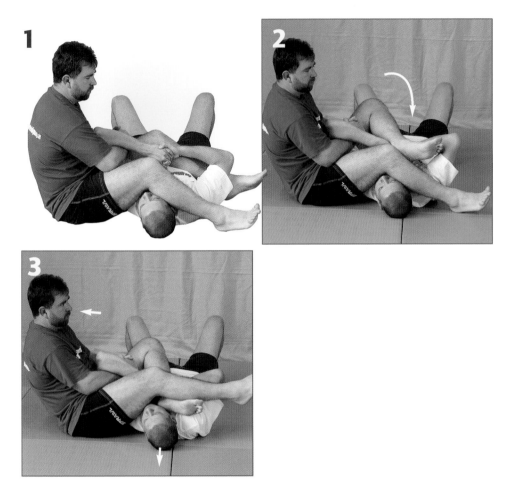

1. D tries to apply a sideways stretched arm lock on A. However, A grasps hold of his own left hand with his free right hand. D's left lower arm is in the crease of A's left elbow and positions his own right lower arm and the right hand holding A's left lower arm close to the left wrist (lock). A blocks this.

2. D now lays, first of all, the left foot (just above the heel) against A's left lower arm close to the wrist...

3. ...and then he lays the right leg (hollow at the back of the knee on the instep) over this.

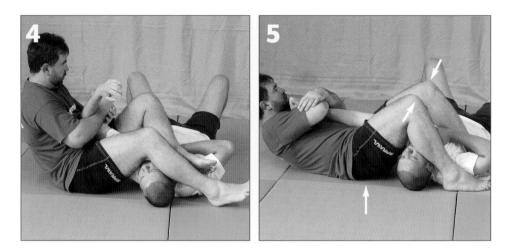

4. A loosens the grip.
5. Now, D can apply the stretched arm lock (Juji Gatame) (A probably surrenders beforehand).

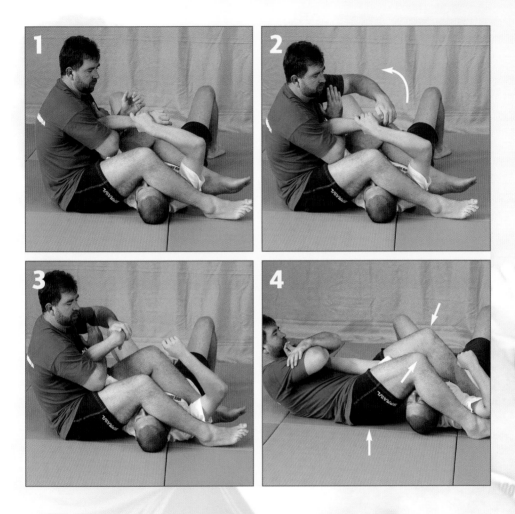

1. D tries to apply a sideways stretched arm lock on A. However, A grasps hold of his own left hand with his free right hand. D's right lower arm is in the crease of A's left elbow. A blocks this.
2. D grasps hold of A's left wrist with his left hand and executes a bent hand lever.
3. Because of this A loosens his grip.
4. D leans backwards, presses his knees together and places both feet underneath A's right arm so that A cannot get at D's toes. D lifts his hips up and pins A's outstretched arm against A's upper body.

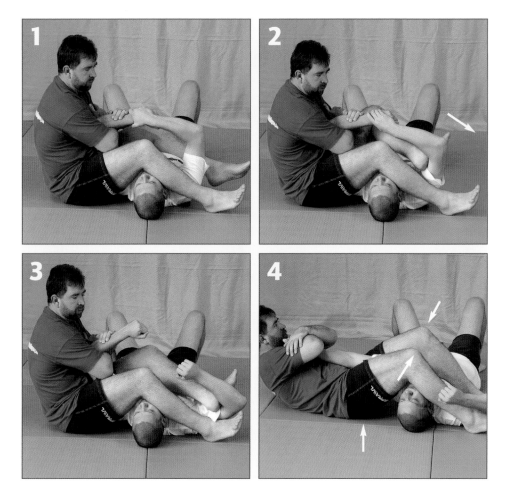

1. D tries to apply a sideways stretched arm lock on A. However, A grasps hold of his own left hand with his free right hand. D's right lower arm is in the crease of A's left elbow and positions his own right lower arm and the right hand holding A's left lower arm close to the left wrist (lock). A blocks this.
2. D places his left foot against A's right upper arm...
3. ...and shoves this away to the rear with a kick so that the grip is freed.
4. D now immobilizes A with a sideways stretched arm lock (Juji Gatame).

Continuation (Variation):

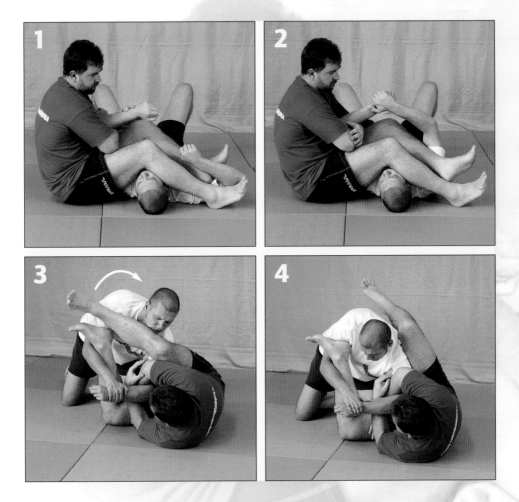

1. If, after A's right arm has been kicked away...
2. ...A grasps round D's left leg and takes hold of his arm again...
3. ...D brings A forward with the legs and lays himself a little over to the left side (for this D pulls A forward a little).
4. D brings his right leg over A's head...

5.   ...angles his left leg and brings it over A's neck.

6.   D takes hold of his own left ankle with his right hand so that A cannot stand up...

7.   ...and lays the hollow at the back of the knee over his left instep...

8.   ...then grasps the left foot with the right hand, pulls it right into the hollow at the back of the knee and chokes A with a triangular lever (Sangaku, Figure Four, Triangle).

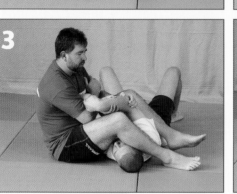

1. D tries to apply a sideways stretched arm lock on A. However, A grasps hold of his own left hand with his free right hand and in such a manner that the two hands each hold the other lower arm. D's right lower arm is in the crease of A's left elbow. A blocks this.

2. D grasps A's right elbow with the left hand, pulls the right arm to the center of A's body...

3. ...so that A loosens his grip.

4. D pins A's left arm against his upper body.

5. D leans backwards, pushes his knees together and places both feet underneath A's right arm so that A cannot get at D's toes. D lifts his hips up and pins A's outstretched arm against A's upper body.

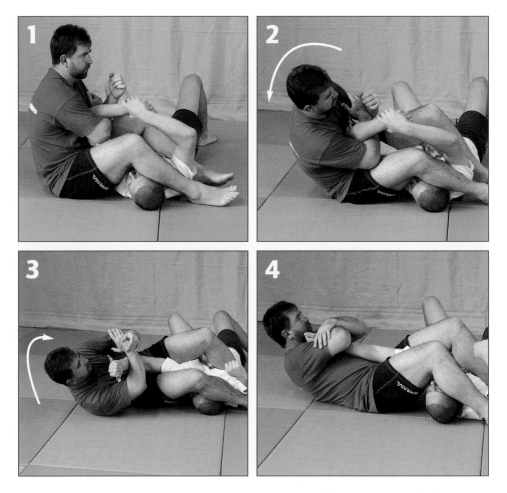

1. D tries to apply a sideways stretched arm lock on A. However, A grasps hold of his own left hand with his free right hand. D's right lower arm is in the crease of A's left elbow. A blocks this.
2. D pulls A's left arm...
3. ...lays himself over on to his right side...
4. ...pulls backwards and breaks A's grip. D ends the combination with a sideways stretched lock.

Escape from the Stretched Arm Lock

1. A tries to apply a sideways stretched lock on D. D holds his left hand firm with his right hand...
2. ...grasps hold of A's outside thigh with the left hand...
3. ...and turns himself over the right shoulder escape himself from the lever.
4. D gets on top of A.
5. D can now circle round A

(counterclockwise) so that D can get into the cross position (side mount) (270°) or clockwise by making a 90° turn into the cross position (side mount).

9.12　Foot and Leg Locks

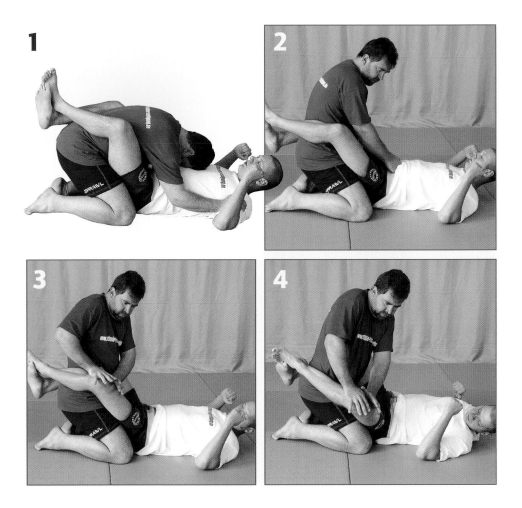

1. D is in A's guard position.
2. D lifts himself up.
3. ...jerks back hard so that his hips come forward. Otherwise A can pull D down by pulling on his legs. D places both hands in the region of the left knee...
4. ...and pushes the leg with an up-and-down movement...

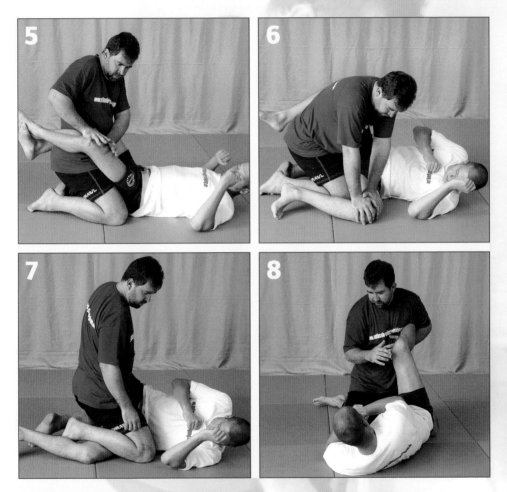

5. ...downwards. If only pressure is applied to the leg, it is very difficult against strong opponents to break the guard. Note: If D, while executing the up-and-down motion on the leg, sags his hips, A can grasp hold of him and pull him back down again.

6. After D has managed to push A's left leg down onto the ground...

7. ...D kneels his right knee down over A's left thigh...

8. ...with A's right leg underneath his left armpit.

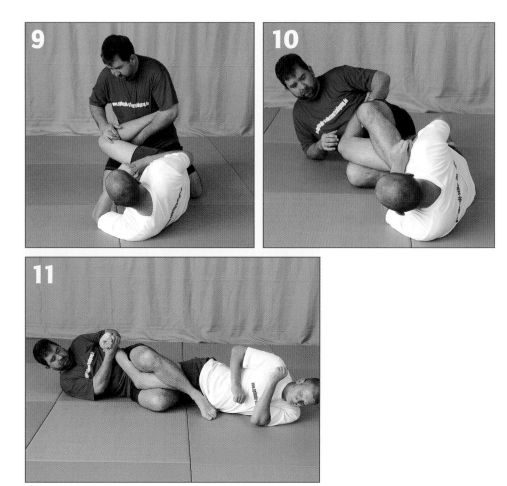

9. A pulls his right leg up a little in order to maintain his distance from D, bends it to the left inside in front of D's upper body...

10. ...and tips D over onto the left side. D uses this movement and swings his left leg round from the outside round A's right leg. D then lays down on his right side and places his foot close alongside A's left hand side...

11. ...brings his left arm to the rear and slides over A's heel from the rear and applies a foot lock (Twister).

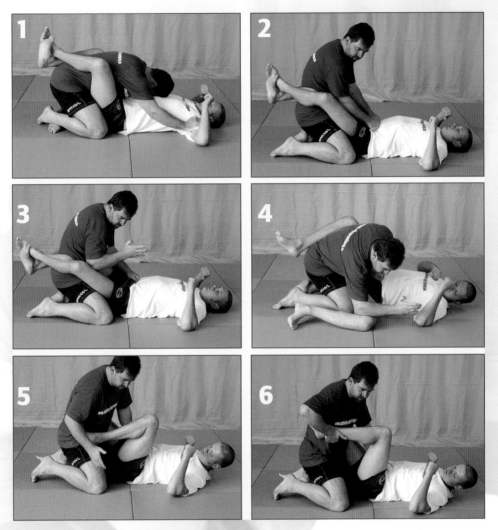

1. D is in A's guard position.
2. D lifts himself up.
3. ...leans back hard so that his hips come forward. Otherwise A can pull D down by pulling on his legs. D presses his right elbow against A's thigh in the region just above the left knee so that A loosens his grip with the legs.
4. After D has pushed A's left leg down onto the ground..
5. ...A lays on his back and immediately places his left leg against D's right groin/hip.
6. D grasps round A's lower leg from the outside with his right...

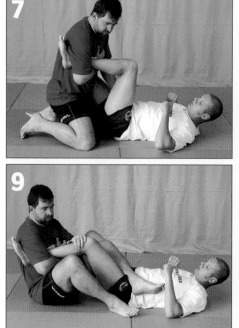

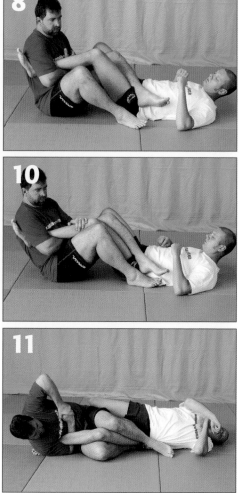

7. ...and pulls the leg up underneath his right armpit and at the same time slides his left leg onto A's thigh. The left arm is underneath A's lower leg and the back of D's right hand is lying on his own chest. It is placed as high up as possible. D is pinning A's right leg with the left arm, by grasping it in the hollow at the back of the right knee with the left hand round from the outside. D now presses himself slightly to the left in order to unweight his right foot...

8. ...and then lets himself fall down to the right side, placing the right foot close to A's right hand side. The right knee is pressing hard against A's thigh so that A's leg is pinned between both of D's legs.

9. D now loosens the pinning action against A's right leg and places the left hand just underneath A's left knee. Then, three movements are carried out in the following sequence:

10. D pulls his own right hand up with the left hand, then lays back...

11. ...stretches his body and turns over clockwise.

1. A is lying on his back and is holding D in a triangular choke (Sangaku, Figure Four, Triangle). However, A has not managed to pull the right arm in the direction of his right groin. Thus the choking action is not effective.
2. D pushes himself up...
3. ...places the left foot on A's right upper arm...
4. ...and then places the right knee against A's coccyx.

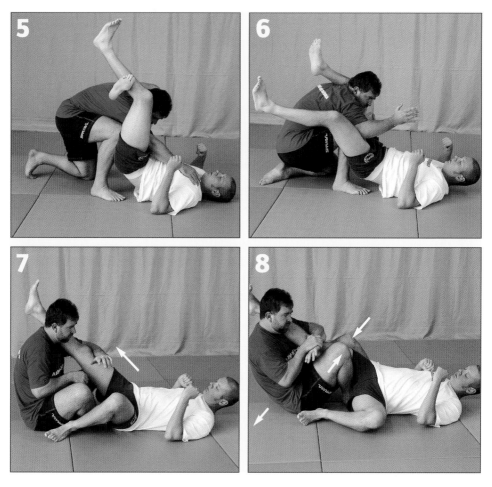

5. D sets himself back (D's right lower leg is now directly in front of A's genital area)...

6. ...and breaks the hold by pressing against A's left thigh with his right elbow/lower arm.

7. D lays the left lower arm just above A's right knee on the thigh...

8. ...grasps his own left hand with his right hand and has placed A's right leg next to the left hand side of the head and pulls A's right leg straight with the arms thereby effecting a stretched leg lock.

1. A is standing opposite D.

2. D fakes an attack at A's head so that A puts his arm up.

3. D protects himself by laying the left hand on his own head – D protects himself by stretching out his left arm (supported by his right hand on his elbow) in the direction of A's head as if to deliver a finger jab, thus covering the whole of his left side. D places his left foot between A's legs, ducks down under his cover kneels on his right knee. D places his left shoulder against A's left thigh and presses his head against the outside of A's left thigh.

4. D grasps round the left thigh at about the height of the knee joint.

5. D places his left lower leg behind A's left heel, presses with his head against the thigh from the outside...

6. ...and pulls A's left leg so that A fall over backwards.

7. As soon as A hits the ground...

8. ...D lays his left foot round A's left foot so that A cannot unhook his left leg from D's hold ...

9. ...brings his right leg out to the right into a position at about right angles to A ...

10. ...adopts the cross position (side mount, Yoko Shio Gatame) and keeps his head down to protect himself from possible strikes.

11. D's left hand is placed between A's legs and the right hand is placed down by the right hand side of A's body.

12. D is holding A's right leg close to his chest with his left arm and supports himself on the ground with his left arm or on A's chest and pushes his own upper body upwards. For this, it is more advantageous to use the arm on the ground, because it provides a more stable triangular support. During this D keeps A's leg held tight to his body.

13. D climbs diagonally over A's upper body with his right leg. For this, D places his right knee on the ground and has laid his right lower leg into A's right groin. D places himself directly next to A so that there is a 45° angle between them.

14. D grasps round the hollow at the back of A's right knee with the left hand, places the left leg between A's legs below the left thigh and leans backwards. D is holding closely round A's right leg and he slides both arms close along A's leg. D executes the leg lever as if wanted to tear the bark from a tree. In the final position A's foot is lying on D's right shoulder.

1. A carries out a bear hug from behind around D's body under the arms.
2. D grasps A's forward leg in both hands...
3. ...sits down onto the thigh...
4. ...and executes a pulled leg action (leg lock).
5. D takes hold of A's right foot round the Achilles tendon and places the right leg about the height of the back of A's knee and turns round 180°...
6. ...forcing A onto his stomach this way.
7. D ends the combination with a bent leg lock.

1. A is standing with his left foot forward. D grasps hold of A's neck with both hands and tries to pull the head down.
2. A resists this and pulls his head up.
3. D uses the energy this provides and lets go of the head and grasps hold of the hollow at the back of A's left knee, places the head against the inside of A's left thigh...
4. ...stands up and lifts A's leg and carefully pulls it between his own legs.

5. D presses with his right shoulder against A's thigh and takes a step turn 90° to the rear...

6. ...thus forcing A to fall over backwards.

7. D pulls up his knee thus executing a bent leg lock and sits on A's left foot. D is blocking A with his left foot by placing it in A's left groin to prevent A being able to stand up.

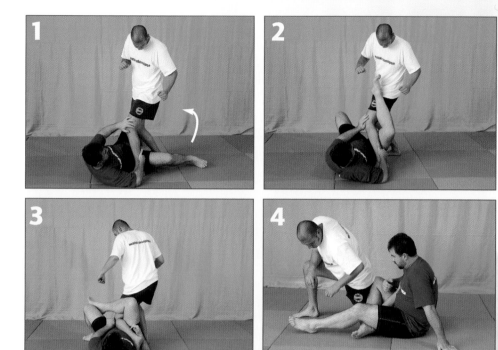

1. A is standing in front of D who is lying on the ground. D's right leg is between A's legs and his left leg is round the outside.

2. D turns himself over to the right so that he is lying almost at right angles to A, swings both legs in the direction of his head and wraps the right leg from the outside round A's left leg...

3. ...swings the legs again downwards...

4. ...forcing A to fall over forwards. D places the right foot into the hollow at the back of the left knee (Sangaku, Figure Four, Triangle)...

5. ...and immobilizes A with a bent leg lock.

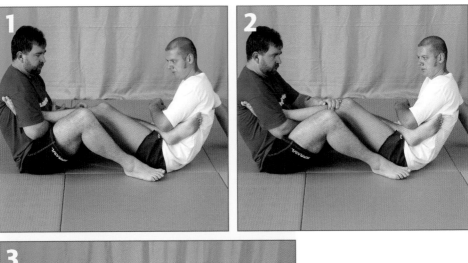

1. A and D are sitting on the floor facing each other. D has hold of A's left foot under his right armpit and pushes his right arm through underneath A's left calf...

2. ...and lays the right hand on top of his own left lower arm. D places the left hand on A's left lower leg...

3. ...pushes his hips forward and leans backwards. In this way he is carrying out a stretched foot lock (leg lock).

Note: It is not a good thing to use this technique on someone who is larger than oneself, because that person could also use the same technique and has the advantage that his legs are longer and thus you can only achieve a small amount of effect.

Escape from Leg Locks

1. A and D are lying on the ground on their backs. A has hold of D's outstretched right leg underneath his armpit and is pinning the leg using his thighs. A's right lower arm is immediately behind the calf and the right hand is lying on his own left lower arm (levered). The left hand is lying on D's right lower leg. A places his right foot under the hollow at the back of D's left knee...

2. ...to turn D to the left.

3. Just as D is round on his stomach...

4. ...he pulls the left leg out of the grasp and stands up.

Note: This technique should not be used when a twisted foot lock is applied (Twister) otherwise D could injure his tendons. This kind of escape movement is designed only for when a normal leg lock has been applied.

If A has hold of the foot very tightly and D cannot pull it out:

1. D lets himself fall down onto the right side and places the left leg on A's buttock muscle near the thigh...
2. ...and pushes against the muscle (or thigh) and rips his leg out of the grasp.

APPENDIX

Literature

On my Internet web pages under www.open-mind-combat.com a list of books can be found. Those interested can gain an overview of the Martial Arts literature. The publishers of this book, Meyer & Meyer, have a large coverage of publications on the Martial Arts – see their Internet web page under www.m-m-sports.com

www.fight-academy.eu

Picture Acknowledgements

Cover Design: Jens Vogelsang, Aachen
Photos: Gabriele Rogall-Zelt

About the Author

Christian Braun, b. 1965

Address:
Peter-Paul-Rubens-Str. 1
67227 Frankenthal
E-Mail: Christian.Braun@open-mind-combat.com
Internet: www.open-mind-combat.com

Requests for information regarding courses, books and private training should be sent to the above address.

Qualifications in Jiu Jitsu:
*   5th Dan Ju-Jutsu, Licensed JJ-Instructor, Trainer 'B' License

Further Qualifications:
*   Head Instructor Open Mind Combat (OMC)
*   Phase 6 and Madunong Guro in the IKAEF under Jeff Espinous and Johan Skalberg
*   Instructor in Progressive Fighting Systems (Jeet Kune Do Concepts) under Paul Vunak
*   Instructor in Luta-Livre License Grade 1 under Andreas Schmidt
*   1st Dan Jiu-Jitsu (German Jiu-Jitsu Association)
*   Phase 2 Jun Fan Gung Fu under Ralf Beckmann

Personal Security:
*   Trainer for personal security for the managing board of a big IT-Company in Baden-Württemberg, Germany.
*   Trainer for personal security of the company MS Event Security in Grünstad, Germany.

Offices held:
*   1990-1991 – Trainer and Press Representative for the Ju-Jutsu Section of the Judo Association for the German State of the Pfalz (Rhineland Palatinate)
*   1999-2003 – Speaker for the Ju-Jutsu Association (Ju-Jutsu Verband Baden e.V.) in matters for Sport for Seniors and the Disabled
*   1992-today – Head of Section in the Turn- und Fechtclub 1861 e.V. (German Gymnastics and Fencing Club 1861)

Organization:

- Speaker on the German National Seminar of the DJJV e.V. (German Ju-Jutsu Association) 2003 and 2004
- Member of the Ju-Jutsu-Leitbildkommission (German Jiu Jitsu Steering Committee) for the DJJV e.V
- Speaker at German National Courses held by the DJJV e.V.
- Speaker in the faculty of JJ Instructors Division of the DJJV e.V.
- Member of the Trainer Team of the Ju-Jutsu Verband Baden e.V.
- Member of the Trainer Team of the DJJV e.V. in the faculty for Sport for the Disabled

Competition Achievements in the Upper Open Weight Classes:

Between 1988-1991 several place results achieved in the Pfalz Individual Championships with 1st Place taken in 1991. Placed in Third Place, three times in the German South-West Individual Championships. 2004, placed in Fourth Place in the Lock and Choke Tournament of the European Luta-Livre-Organization in the Upper Open Weight Class. In January 2005 in Karlsruhe, placed in Second Place in the Submissao Grappling Challenge. In February 2005 in Cologne, placed in Second Place in the Luta-Livre German Individual Championships in the Weight Class +99 kg.

Christian Braun
Self-Defense against Knife Attacks

Techniques for the defense against knife attacks are not only of interest for martial artists in the various disciplines. Everyone who is looking for effective ways to defend himself against these attacks in all kinds of situations will find detailed instructions in this book. In numerous exercise forms, illustrated with about 1700 color photos, this book describes the use of distracting techniques, concepts to control and secure the knife-holding hand, and how to disarm the attacker.

c. 270 pages, full-color print
1700 photos and illustrations
Paperback, 6$^1/2$" x 9$^1/4$"
ISBN 978-1-84126-198-0
c.$ 19.95 US/$ 26.95 CDN
£ 12.95 UK/€ 16.95

Helmut Kogel
Kobudo – Bo-Jutsu
Technique – Training – Katas

The beginner will find a systematic introduction into the basics of Bo fighting techniques. The advanced student will get important insights into training instructions and will learn detailed patterns of the so-called special forms, which means traditional Okinawan Bo-katas. The content of "Kobudo – Bo Jutsu" is based on the experience which the author gained during numerous studies in Japan and Okinawa. Therefore, authentic Kobudo is presented in this book.

172 pages, full-color print
500 photos and illustrations
Paperback, 5$^3/4$" x 8$^1/4$"
ISBN 978-1-84126-172-0
$ 17.95 US/$ 25.95 CDN
£ 12.95 UK/€ 16.95

MEYER & MEYER

MEYER & MEYER distribution@m-m-sports.com• www.m-m-sports.com

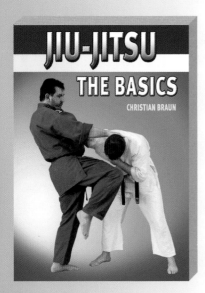

Christian Braun
Jiu-Jitsu
The Basics

In almost a thousand step by step photographs, the Jiu-Jitsu techniques are explained, so that Jiu-Jitsuka of any standard will be able to follow them and use them. Another feature of "Jiu-Jitsu – The Basics" are lessons concerning lokking, throwing, striking and kicking techniques, as well as an introduction to self-defense in groundwork. This book on the basics will also provide the trainer with a comprehensive reference book.

200 pages, full-color print
900 photos and illustrations
Paperback, 5 3/4" x 8 1/4"
ISBN 978-1-84126-171-3
$ 17.95 US/$ 25.95 CDN
£ 12.95 UK/€ 16.95

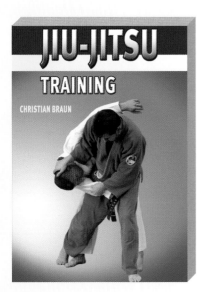

Christian Braun
Jiu-Jitsu
Training

Jiu-Jitsu Training moves on from the author's first book, Jiu-Jitsu – The Basics, and is directed at every Jiu-Jitsuka who has learned the basics and wants to improve. In more than a thousand illustrative photographs, the techniques are explained step by step. The book covers the basic positions, techniques and combinations. It Includes an introduction to self-defense in groundwork.
An effective preparation for a grading test and a comprehensive reference book!

264 pages, full-color print
1431 photos and illustrations
Paperback, 6 1/2" x 9 1/4"
ISBN 978-1-84126-179-9
$ 19.95 US/$ 26.95 CDN
£ 14.95 UK/€ 18.95

MEYER & MEYER distribution@m-m-sports.com • www.m-m-sports.com

MEYER
&MEYER
SPORT

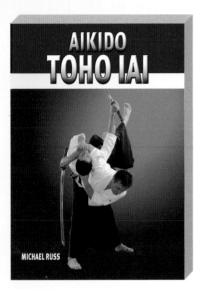

Michael Russ
Aikido Toho Iai

Training Aikido without using the sword is not enough. This book introduces for the first time a system founded by Nishio Sensei called Aikido Toho Iai, which is the connection between the art of sword drawing and Aikido technique. The sword is the origin of the Aikido technique, and this book shows how to use it in the right way.
In more than 500 illustrative photographs, the techniques are explained step by step.

264 pages, full-color print
700 photos and illustrations
Paperback, 5³/₄" x 8¹/₄"
ISBN 978-1-84126-183-6
c. $ 19.95 US/$ 26.95 CDN
£ 14.95 UK/€ 18.95

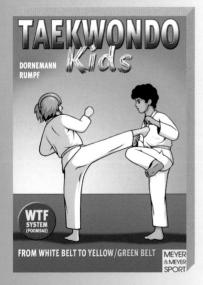

Dornemann/Rumpf
Taekwondo Kids
From White Belt to Yellow/Green Belt

Taekwondo Kids provides us with the first practical guide to the Korean Martial Arts System of Taekwondo and has been specially written with children and youths in mind. It serves as an accompaniment to training as well as providing an introduction to this particular sport. Using simple easily understood language and numerous appropriate illustrations suitable for children and youths, all the exercises can be carried out or practiced further without any difficulty.

c. 128 pages, full-color print
200 drawings
Paperback, 6¹/₂" x 9¹/₄"
ISBN 978-1-84126-214-7
c. $ 14.95 US/$ 19.95 CDN
£ 9.95 UK/€ 12.95

MEYER & MEYER distribution@m-m-sports.com• www.m-m-sports.com